Holly Chantler is an award winning internationally recognised mental capacity solicitor. She advises on complex property and affairs and health and welfare matters, frequently involving safeguarding concerns, disputed capacity, high-value estates and cross-border issues. Holly is a founding director of the Professional Deputies Forum and a director of The Association of Lifetime Lawyers and works regularly with government stakeholders to help shape both practice and policy in this field.

Holly is the author of 'A Practical Guide to Assessing Mental Capacity' and 'A Practical Guide to the Court of Protection' and a contributing author to the Law Society's 'Elderly Client Handbook' and 'Finance & Law for the Older Client' (LexisNexis). She lectures extensively nationally and internationally and is a regular commentator on capacity and safeguarding issues. Her work has been recognised through independent rankings and national awards. This book builds on her practical experience of advising in complex domestic and international capacity cases, and her long-standing focus on translating difficult law into clear, usable guidance for practitioners.

Mental Capacity Law in England and Wales: Recognition and Enforcement of Protective Measures and Private Mandates

Mental Capacity Law in England and Wales: Recognition and Enforcement of Protective Measures and Private Mandates

Holly Chantler

Law Brief Publishing

Published 2026 by Law Brief Publishing, an imprint of Law Brief Publishing Ltd
30 The Parks
Minehead
Somerset
TA24 8BT

www.lawbriefpublishing.com

Paperback: 978-1-918241-32-7

PREFACE

This book is intended as a practical guide for practitioners advising on mental capacity matters with an international element. Cross-border issues arise with increasing frequency in Court of Protection and private client work, whether through international families, overseas assets, foreign protective measures or the movement of adults who lack capacity between jurisdictions. The interaction between domestic capacity law and principles of private international law can be complex and the consequences of getting it wrong can be significant for both clients and advisers. This book aims to provide clear, structured guidance to support informed and confident decision-making in this challenging area.

The text focuses on the law of England and Wales and, in particular, the Mental Capacity Act 2005, the Court of Protection Rules and relevant case law. It applies case law, procedural rules and practical experience to explore recognition and enforcement of foreign protective measures, the treatment of overseas powers of attorney, jurisdiction, habitual residence and the options available where formal recognition is not achievable. Throughout, the emphasis is on practical application rather than theory, with worked examples and checklists designed to assist practitioners at the point of need. The book uses fictional case studies to support the legal points raised.

The law is stated as correct as at 14 April 2026. Given the pace of judicial development in this field, readers should always consider whether there have been subsequent legislative changes or reported decisions before relying on the guidance in any live matter. Nothing in this book is intended to constitute advice on foreign law, and practitioners should continue to seek advice from appropriately qualified advisers in the relevant jurisdiction where necessary.

Holly Chantler
April 2026

CONTENTS

CHAPTER ONE

INTRODUCTION

Introduction

This book offers a practical and accessible guide for practitioners navigating the increasingly complex interaction between mental capacity law and cross-border issues. It will only consider the position with regard to adults.

As international mobility grows and families, assets and care arrangements extend beyond national boundaries, advisers are more frequently required to consider issues of jurisdiction, recognition and enforcement of foreign protective measures and powers of attorney. This book will consider the core principles and procedures relating to foreign protective measures, private mandates, deputyship applications and one-off orders, applying the legal framework contained in the Hague Convention on the International Protection of Adults (Hague 35), the Mental Capacity Act 2005 and evolving case law of the Court of Protection. It will also consider the practical and legal implications when an incapacitated adult moves abroad or acquires ties to multiple jurisdictions. Designed as a clear roadmap through a challenging area of law, the book will provide professionals with confidence to address cross-border capacity issues effectively and to anticipate the reforms still to come.

Convention on the International Production of Adults ("the Convention")

The Hague Convention of 13 January 2000 on the International Protection of Adults, also known as Hague 35, was signed by the United Kingdom on 1 April 2003. It was subsequently ratified but only in respect of Scotland and as such, it is not (yet) in force in England and Wales. Currently the only Contracting States are European[1].

The Convention makes provision for the mutual recognition of protective measures (discussed later) by Contracting States. It only relates to adults; Hague 34 applies to children until they reach the age of 18.

Article 1

(1) This Convention applies to the protection in international situations of adults who, by reason of an impairment or insufficiency of their personal faculties, are not in a position to protect their interests.

(2) Its objects are –

a. to determine the State whose authorities have jurisdiction to take measures directed to the protection of the person or property of the adult;

b. to determine which law is to be applied by such authorities in exercising their jurisdiction;

c. to determine the law applicable to representation of the adult;

d. to provide for the recognition and enforcement of such measures of protection in all Contracting States;

---

1 The Current contracting States can be found at https://www.hcch.net/en/instruments/conventions/status-table/?cid=71

e. to establish such co-operation between the authorities of the Contracting States as may be necessary in order to achieve the purposes of this Convention.

Article 22 of the Convention requires a protective measure in place in respect of a protected adult issued in a contracting state ("State A") to be recognised by operation of law in another contracting state ("State B"). An application may be made by "any interested person" under Article 23 for recognition by State B of a protective measure issued by State A.

As mentioned above, the Convention has only been ratified by the United Kingdom in relation to Scotland. It is due to be ratified in relation to England and Wales, and whilst it had anticipated this would be in the near future, it is a project that continues to be pushed back by the Ministry of Justice.

As the Convention has yet to be ratified in England and Wales, it will not be considered in any detail in this book but practitioners should be aware that there is an intention to ratify and continue to review the situation.

SUMMARY

- The United Kingdom signed the Convention on 1 April 2003
- It has been ratified only for Scotland, not for England and Wales and is therefore not yet in force in England and Wales
- Practitioners should be aware of the Convention and that it is intended to be ratified in relation to England and Wales

The legal framework in England and Wales

The mental capacity legal framework in England and Wales is governed by the Mental Capacity Act 2005[2] ("the Act"), the Court of Protection Rules 2017[3], practice directions[4], Mental Capacity Act 2005 Code of Practice[5] and case law. Scotland and Northern Ireland have a distinct legal system from England and Wales and these will not be considered in this book.

Section 45 of the Act established the Court of Protection. It is a distinct court, only able to make decisions on behalf of someone who lacks capacity to take a particular decision or in relation to such a person (referred to in the legislation as "P"). It was, however, determined in *United Lincolnshire Hospitals NHS Trust v CD*[6] (and has been confirmed in subsequent case law) that the court has, in exceptional circumstances, the power to make an anticipatory declaration of lawfulness pursuant to section 15(1)(c) of the Act, contingent on the incapacitated person (known as "P") losing capacity.

Most applications made to the Court of Protection are in relation to the property or welfare of persons habitually resident in England and Wales. However, the Act does contain provisions relating to the power of the court in situations where a person lacking capacity to make decisions is habitually resident outside of England and Wales.

---

2 https://www.legislation.gov.uk/ukpga/2005/9

3 https://www.legislation.gov.uk/uksi/2017/1035/contents

4 https://www.judiciary.uk/guidance-and-resources/court-of-protection-practice-directions/

5 https://www.gov.uk/government/publications/mental-capacity-act-code-of-practice

6 [2019] EWCOP 24

Notwithstanding that the United Kingdom has not ratified the Convention in respect of England and Wales, it has implemented the terms of the Convention by virtue of section 63 of and Schedule 3 to the Mental Capacity Act 2005. The Act is only applicable in England and Wales and is the relevant statutory framework for practitioners to consider.

63 International Protection of Adults

Schedule 3 –

(a) gives effect in England and Wales to the Convention on the International Protection of Adults signed at the Hague on 14th January 2000 (Cm. 5881) (in so far as this Act does not otherwise do so), and

(b) makes related provision as to the private international law of England and Wales.

Schedule 3 therefore contains two sets of provisions:

1. The first set of provisions will incorporate the Convention into English domestic law but only once the Convention has been brought into effect (paragraph 35 of Schedule 3 to the Act).

2. The second set of provisions are in force but are independent of the Convention. These provisions establish a set of rules for the recognition and enforcement in England and Wales of foreign protective measures, whether or not the foreign state has signed the Convention or if they have a reciprocal arrangement to the jurisdiction of England and Wales (section 63 of the Act).

For the purposes of this book, the focus will be on the second set of provision as the Convention has yet to be ratified (and therefore the first set of provisions are currently not in effect).

SUMMARY

- The legal framework in England and Wales can be found in the Mental Capacity Act 2005, Court of Protection Rules 2017, practice directions, the Code of Practice and case law

- The Court of Protection makes decisions for or in relation to persons who lack mental capacity. Such persons are known as P

- Most cases involve people habitually resident in England and Wales, but the Act also covers situations where a person lacking capacity lives outside the jurisdiction

- Notwithstanding the Convention has yet to be ratified, section 63 and Schedule 3 MCA 2005 still implement the principles of the Convention

Jurisdiction of the Court of Protection

The scope of the jurisdiction of the Court of Protection is set out in paragraph 7(1) of Schedule 3 to the Act.

Scope of jurisdiction

7 (1) The court may exercise its functions under this Act (in so far as it cannot otherwise do so) in relation to –

(a) an adult habitually resident in England and Wales,

(b) an adult's property in England and Wales,

(c) an adult present in England and Wales or who has property there, if the matter is urgent, or

(a) an adult present in England and Wales, if a protective measure which is temporary and limited in its effect to England and Wales is proposed in relation to him.

Additional powers to recognise and enforce foreign protective measures are set out in Part 4 of Schedule 3 to the Act (paragraphs 19-25). These will be considered later in the book.

The domestic definition of "adult" is set out in paragraph 4 of Schedule 3 to the Act.

Adults with incapacity

4 (1) 'Adult' means (subject to sub-paragraph 2) a person who –

(a) as a result of an impairment or insufficiency of his personal faculties, cannot protect his interests, and

(b) has reached 16

(2) But 'adult' does not include a child to whom either of the following applies...

(a) the Convention on Jurisdiction, Applicable Law, Recognition, Enforcement and Co-Operation in respect of Parental Responsibility and Measures for the Protection of Children that was signed at The Hague on 19 October 1996;

(b) ....'

It will be noted the discrepancy between the definition in paragraph 4 of the Act of an adult being 16, unless Hague 34 applies, rather than the Convention which relates to those having attained the age of 18. This issue was considered in *Irwin Mitchell Trust Corporation v KS & Ors*[7]. In this matter, the Court of Protection considered the discharge of a deputy appointed in England and Wales in relation to KS, a young person under 16, who had substantial assets in England but had become habitually resident in India. The Act does not apply to under 16s in relation to jurisdiction issues. Instead, the Court of Protection would have sought to rely on Hague 34 but India is not a party. The explanatory report to Hague 34 (the Largarde Report) states that a non-contracting state should recognise the measure taken in the previous state before the child changed their habitual residence. Legal advice taken in India suggested

7 [2025] EWCOP 7

that both England and Wales and India had jurisdiction, HHJ Hilder determined that the Court of Protection retained jurisdiction, although it may have been different if an Indian deputy equivalent had been appointed or if no deputy had ever been appointed in England and Wales. The issue would fall away upon KS attaining 16.

Property

64 (1) In this Act – .....

"property" includes any thing in action and any interest in real or personal property,

SUMMARY

- Paragraph 7(1) of Schedule 3 to the Act sets out the Court of Protection's jurisdiction
- Part 4 of Schedule 3 to the Act (paragraphs 19–25) gives the court additional powers to recognise and enforce foreign protective measures
- The domestic definition of an "adult" is set out in paragraph 4 of Schedule 3 to the Act and is different to the Convention definition (16, not 18)

Inherent jurisdiction

Even if the Court of Protection determines that it does not have jurisdiction pursuant to paragraph 7(1) of Schedule 3 to the Act, the High Court (separate from the Court of Protection) can exercise its inherent jurisdiction outside of the Act. It should, however, be applied with caution and *"not used in an unprincipled and unlimited manner, and in particular one which cuts across a statutory scheme which necessarily reflects Parliamentary intent"* (paragraph 32 of *DL v A Local Authority*[8]). In practice it is unlikely that the court will consider it does not have jurisdiction under the Act but can exercise its inherent jurisdiction.

SUMMARY

- If the Court of Protection has no jurisdiction, the High Court may still act using its inherent jurisdiction
- The High Court should not use inherent jurisdiction in an unprincipled or excessive manner
- In practice it is rare for the High Court to exercise its inherent jurisdiction in this area

8 [2012] EWCA Civ 253

CHAPTER TWO

PROTECTIVE MEASURES

Protective measures

The domestic definition of protective measure is set out in paragraph 5 of Schedule 3 to the Act.

Protective measures

5 (1) 'Protective measure' means a measure directed to the protection of the person or property of an adult; and it may deal in particular with any of the following –

(a) the determination of incapacity and the institution of a protective regime,

(b) placing the adult under the protection of an appropriate authority,

(c) guardianship, curatorship or any corresponding system,

(d) the designation and functions of a person having charge of the adult's person or property, or representing or otherwise helping him,

(e) placing the adult in a place where protection can be provided,

(f) administering, conserving or disposing of the adult's property,

(g) authorising a specific intervention for the protection of the person or property of the adult.

For practical purposes, a protective measure essentially means the equivalent of a Court of Protection order made in a foreign court.

Recognition

19 (1) A protective measure taken in relation to an adult under the law of a country other than England and Wales is to be recognised in England and Wales if it was taken on the ground that the adult is habitually resident in the other country.

(2) A protective measure taken in relation to an adult under the law of a Convention country other than England and Wales is to be recognised in England and Wales if it was taken on a ground mentioned in Chapter 2 (jurisdiction). [Not currently in force]

(3) But the court may disapply this paragraph in relation to a measure if it thinks that—

(a) the case in which the measure was taken was not urgent,

(b) the adult was not given an opportunity to be heard, and

(c) that omission amounted to a breach of natural justice.

(4) It may also disapply this paragraph in relation to a measure if it thinks that

(a) recognition of the measure would be manifestly contrary to public policy,

(b) the measure would be inconsistent with a mandatory provision of the law of England and Wales, or

(c) the measure is inconsistent with one subsequently taken, or recognised, in England and Wales in relation to the adult.

(5) And the court may disapply this paragraph in relation to a measure taken under the law of a Convention country in a matter to which Article 33 applies, if the court thinks that that Article has not been complied with in connection with that matter.

20 (1) An interested person may apply to the court for a declaration as to whether a protective measure taken under the law of a country other than England and Wales is to be recognised in England and Wales.

(2) No permission is required for an application to the court under this paragraph.

Enforcement

22 (1) An interested person may apply to the court for a declaration as to whether a protective measure taken under the law of, and enforceable in, a country other than England and Wales is enforceable, or to be registered, in England and Wales in accordance with Court of Protection Rules.

> (2) The court must make the declaration if –
>
> (a) the measure comes within sub-paragraph (1) or (2) of paragraph 19, and
>
> (b) the paragraph is not disapplied in relation to it as a result of sub-paragraph (3), (4) or (5).
>
> (3) A measure to which a declaration under this paragraph relates is enforceable in England and Wales as if it were a measure of like effect taken by the court.

An order to reciprocate a foreign protective measure may therefore be sought under Schedule 3 from the Court of Protection by one or more of the following:

i) an application for a declaration under paragraph 20(1) that the measure is recognised in England and Wales;

ii) an application for a declaration under paragraph 22(1) that the measure is enforceable in England and Wales;

iii) an application for a declaration under paragraph 22(1) that the measure is to be registered in England and Wales in accordance with the Court of Protection Rules 2017.

The Court of Protection Rules 2017 do not provide for registration of foreign protective measures and as such, the third option is not (currently) applicable.

Whilst there may be some circumstances where recognition alone is sufficient, in most cases (and in particular in relation to welfare issues), enforcement will also be required. In practice, the terms recognition and enforcement are conflated.

Applications for recognition and/or enforcement are complex – Mostyn J in *Re SV*[9] identified 22 separate questions the Court must address in order to be satisfied of numerous conditions before declarations can be made (see Appendix 1). Theis J in *Argyll and Bute Council v RF*[10] stated that the checklist should be updated to include the additional conditions identified in this decision and that of Poole J in *Aberdeenshire Council v SF, EF and Sunderland City Council*[11] and *Re PQ*[12]. These have been added at Appendix 1 and should be used as a checklist for practitioners when considering making an application for recognition and/or enforcement of a protective measure.

SUMMARY

- A protective measure means any step taken to protect an adult or their property
- In practice, a protective measure is likely to be a foreign equivalent of a Court of Protection order
- A foreign protective measure must be recognised in England and Wales if the adult was habitually resident in the country that made the order, unless the court decides not to recognise it (for reasons such as lack of urgency, breach of natural justice, public policy concerns, or conflict with English law)

---

9 [2022] EWCOP 52

10 [2025] EWCOP 12

11 [2024] EWCOP 10

12 [2024] EWCOP 41

- An interested person can apply to the Court of Protection for a declaration of recognition (paragraph 20 of Schedule 3 to the Act) or enforcement (paragraph 22 of Schedule 3 to the Act) of the foreign measure; if granted, the order is treated as if it were made by the Court of Protection

- Applications for recognition/enforcement are complex, and judges have developed detailed checklists (e.g., *Re SV, Argyll and Bute Council v RF, Aberdeenshire Council v SF, Re PQ*) that practitioners should use when considering and preparing such applications

Habitual residence

As mentioned previously, the Court of Protection has jurisdiction pursuant to paragraph 7(1) of Schedule 3 to the Act if the adult is habitually resident in England and Wales.

Habitual residence under the Act has the same meaning as that applied in other instruments such as the 1996 Hague Convention on the International Protection of Children[13] (Hague 34). It is therefore a question of fact (see *Re MN*[14] and *A v A (Children: Habitual Residence*[15])).

There is extensive case law considering the issue of habitual residence and a number of principles can be identified:

- Habitual residence is to be assessed by reference to all the circumstances as they exist at the time of the assessment (*Re R*

---

13 https://www.hcch.net/en/instruments/conventions/full-text/?cid=70

14 [2010] EWHC 1926 (fam)

15 [2014] AC 1

(Children)[16]) although in *Re QD (Habitual Residence (No 2)*[17] as a result of delays in determining the matter due to the Coronavirus pandemic, the parties agreed they would not argue that passage of time would result in a change of habitual residence.

- An adult can only have one habitual residence for the purposes of the Convention (and, presumably, Schedule 3 of the Act), and may in some circumstances have none.

- For an adult who had, but has subsequently lost, capacity to decide where they wish to live, their habitual residence will remain that of the country in which they were habitually resident at the point they lost capacity. It is possible for their habitual residence to change if they are moved to another country if it is not as a result of any wrongdoing on the part of the third party responsible for the person's care and wellbeing.

- If a change of habitual residence is claimed, the authorities will consider the circumstances of the move itself and the circumstances under which the adult is now residing (in particular whether the move is considered a permanent arrangement). It may be appropriate to consider how settled the adult appears to be and whether they are expressing any wishes and feelings about the placement (see *An English Local Authority v SW*[18]).

- Where an adult has been wrongfully removed, it may be possible for their habitual residence to change if there is subsequent endorsement by the responsible administrative of judicial

16 [2016] AC 76

17 [2020] EWCOP 14

18 [2014] EWCOP 43

authorities of the country of habitual residence and/or all those family members and carers properly interested in the case.

- The passage of a sufficiently long period of time could, in and of itself, effect a change in habitual residence even if the original removal was wrongful (see *AB v XS*[19]). There is no judicial authority as to what constitutes the necessary period of time but Hague 34 (which relates to children) suggests that one year might be sufficient.

- If an adult has never had capacity to decide where to live, their habitual residence at 18 will be that which they had immediately prior to that age. It is possible for their habitual residence to subsequently change.

- The assessment of habitual residence will always be by reference to the facts at the time of assessment.

- The burden of proof will always lie upon the person asserting the change of habitual residence.

- The degree of integration is an overarching summary or question rather than the sole or primary factor in the determination of habitual residence (*An English Local Authority v SW*[20]).

- Habitual residence can in principle be lost and another acquired on the same day (*Re PO (Court of Protection: Jurisdiction)*[21]).

---

19 [2021] EWCOP 57

20 [2014] EWCOP 43

21 [2014] Fam 197 (CP)

- If the incapacitated adult was removed unlawfully then it is unlikely that the person's habitual residence will have changed (*Re MN*[22]).

- Habitual residence can be lost and another acquired without the need for a court order or other formal process, such as the appointment of an attorney or deputy (*Re PO (Court of Protection: Jurisdiction*[23]).

- The fact that the person effecting the move has formed a subjective view or considers it a "crime of necessity" to remove the person in their best interests, it is not sufficient to prevent the move from being wrongful (or a change of habitual residence to occur) (*Re QD (Jurisdiction: Habitual Residence) (No 1)*[24]).

- Where the person is settled in a country and wished to live there, removal to another country (especially if done with no authority) is unlikely to result in a change in habitual residence (*Re A (Habitual Residence)*[25]

A useful summary to determining habitual residence was set out in *The Health Service Executive of Ireland v IM & Anor*[26]:

> "28. "Habitual residence" is defined in neither the MCA nor the Convention. In *An English Local Authority v SW and Others* [2014] EWCOP 43, Moylan J (as he then was) held that the meaning to be given to habitual residence in the

---

22 [2010] EWHC 1926 (Fam)

23 [2014] Fam 197 (CP)

24 [2019] EWCOP 56

25 [2025] EWCOP 22

26 [2020] EWCOP 51

context of the Convention and the MCA should be the same as in other family law instruments such as the 1996 Hague Child Protection Convention and Council Regulation EC 2201/2003 (Brussels IIA) though he also acknowledged that different factors will be relevant and will bear differential weight (see [64]-[65]).

29. Thus, habitual residence is to be determined in accordance with the guidance given by the Supreme Court and the Court of Justice of the European Union in a number of recent cases. The following principles are key:

a) Habitual residence is a question of fact and not a legal concept such as domicile (*A v A (Children: Habitual Residence*) [2014] AC 1 at [54]);

b) The test adopted by the ECJ is the "place which reflects some degree of integration by the child in a social and family environment". The child's physical presence should not be temporary or intermittent (*Proceedings brought by A* (Case C-523/07) [2010] Fam 42 at [38]);

c) Consideration needs to be given to conditions and reasons for the child's stay in the state in question (*Mercredi v Chaffe* (Case C-497/10PPU) [2012] Fam 22 at [48]);

d) The essentially factual and individual nature of the enquiry should not be glossed with legal concepts which would produce a different result from that which the factual enquiry would produce (see *A v A* above at [54]);

e) Both objective and subjective factors need to be considered. Rather than consider a person's wishes or intentions, it is better to think in terms of the reasons why a person is in a particular place and his or her perception of the situation while there – their state of mind (*Re LC (Children)* [2014] AC 1038 at [60]);

f) It is the stability of the residence that is important, not whether it is of a permanent character (*Re R (Children)* [2016] AC 76 at [16]); and

g) Habitual residence is to be assessed by reference to all the circumstances as they exist at the time of assessment (*FT v MM* [2019] EWHC 935 (Fam) at [13])".

SUMMARY

- Habitual residence determines whether the Court of Protection has jurisdiction under Schedule 3 to the Act
- It is a question of fact, assessed using the same approach as in other international family-law instruments such as Hague 34
- A person can have only one habitual residence and in rare situations may have none
- Habitual residence usually stays where it was when the adult lost capacity, but it can change if they move abroad lawfully and settle there
- Wrongful or unlawful removal makes a change of habitual residence unlikely, though a long enough passage of time may still shift it

Applications for determination of habitual residence

Applications for determinations of habitual residence are not Schedule 3 applications and instead must be made pursuant to sections 15 and/or 16 of the Act.

Considerations to be made by the Court of Protection following an application for recognition and/or enforcement of a protective measure

A decision to recognise a foreign protective measure is not a best interests decision (*Re MN*[27]). In reaching its decision, the Court of Protection is entitled to conduct a limited review, and to apply a light touch (*Health Service Executive of Ireland v PA & Ors*[28] at [96]).

Factors the Court of Protection may consider following an application for recognition and/or enforcement include:

1. The joinder of P

   Where the application is being made without opposition it will be rare for P to be joined to the proceedings (*Re SV*[29]and *Health Service Executive of Ireland v CNWL*[30]).

2. Whether P was heard in the foreign proceedings

   If the proceedings were not held on an urgent basis and if P was denied the opportunity to be heard then paragraph 19(3)(c) of the Act allows recognition to be withheld on the grounds of natural

---

27 [2010] EWHC 1926 (fam)

28 [2015] EWCOP 38

29 [2022] EWCOP 52

30 [2015] EWCOP 48

justice (see *Aberdeenshire Council v SF & Ors*[31] and *Argyll and Bute Council v RF*[32]).

3. Whether P has capacity under sections 2 and 3 of the Act to make the decision in question.

If P is to be joined, the court must then consider whether the adult has capacity to conduct the proceedings (applying sections 2 and 3 of the Act and relevant case law, in particular *Masterman-Lister v Brutton and Co*[33]).

4. Whether the measure is inconsistent with a mandatory provision of the law of England and Wales.

5. Whether the measure entails a deprivation of liberty for the purposes of Article 4 of the European Convention on Human Rights ("ECHR").

The Court must be satisfied:

i) Objective medical expertise has established that P's medical disorder is of a type and degree that warrants P's compulsory confinement (see *Winterwerp v Netherlands* (1979)[34] at [39], *Health Service Executive of Ireland v PA & Ors*[35] at [89] and

31 (No. 2) [2024] EWCOP 10

32 [2025] EWCOP 12 (T3)

33 [2002] EWCA Civ 1889

34 2 EHRR 387

35 [2015] EWCOP 38

[96], *Health Service Executive of Ireland v CNWL*[36] at [17], and *Health Service Executive of Ireland v Moorgate* [2020][37] at [35]);

ii) P has the right in the foreign country to challenge the detention (see *Health Service Executive of Ireland v PA & Ors* at [97]);

iii) The detention is regularly reviewed by the foreign court.

SUMMARY

- Recognising a foreign protective measure is not a best-interests decision.
- The court only carries out a limited, light-touch review
- The court may consider whether P needs to be joined, though this is rare in unopposed applications
- The court considers whether P had an opportunity to be heard in the foreign proceedings; if not, recognition may be refused for breach of natural justice
- The court must ensure any deprivation of liberty meets ECHR Article 5 safeguards: medical evidence justifying confinement, a right to challenge detention abroad and regular reviews by the foreign court

36 [2022] EWCOP 52

37 EWCOP 12

Refusal to recognise and/or enforce a foreign protective measure

Section 19(3) of Schedule 3 to the Act sets out the circumstances in which the Court of Protection may refuse to recognise a foreign protective measure.

> 19. (1) A protective measure taken in relation to an adult under the law of a country other than England and Wales is to be recognised in England and Wales if it was taken on the ground that the adult is habitually resident in the other country.
>
> (2) A protective measure taken in relation to an adult under the law of a Convention country other than England and Wales is to be recognised in England and Wales if it was taken on the ground mentioned in Chapter 2 (jurisdiction).
>
> (3) But the court may disapply this paragraph in relation to a measure if it thinks that –
>
> (a) the case in which the measure was taken was not urgent,
>
> (b) the adult was not given an opportunity to be heard, and
>
> (c) that omission amounted to a breach of natural justice.
>
> (4) It may also disapply this paragraph in relation to a measure if it thinks that –
>
> (a) recognition of the measure would be manifestly contrary to public policy,

(b) the measure would be inconsistent with a mandatory provision of the law in England and Wales, or

(c) the measure is inconsistent with one subsequently taken, or recognised, in England and Wales in relation to the adult.

(5) And the court may disapply this paragraph in relation to a measure taken under the law of a Convention country in a matter to which Article 33 applies, if the court thinks that the Article has not been complied with in connection with that matter.

The Court of Protection does refuse to recognise foreign protective measures; an application is not guaranteed to succeed. See in particular *Aberdeenshire Council v SF & Ors*[38] where the court refused to recognise an order made in Scotland on the grounds of natural justice because the incapacitated adult had not had an opportunity to be heard as part of the original (Scottish) proceedings and *Argyll and Bute Council v RF*[39] where Theis J refused to recognise an order on the same grounds. In *AB*[40] the court found that it would be against the policy of judicial comity to recognise and enforce a US guardianship order on the basis of the mother's actions (the US appointed guardian).

38 (No. 2) [2024] EWCOP 10

39 [2025] EWCOP 12 (T3)

40 [2020] EWCOP 47

SUMMARY

- The Court of Protection must recognise a foreign protective measure if the adult was habitually resident in the country that made it, unless certain exceptions apply
- The court can refuse recognition if the case was not urgent, the adult was not given a chance to be heard and this amounted to a breach of natural justice
- Recognition may also be refused if it is against public policy, inconsistent with mandatory English law or conflicts with a later measure made or recognised in England and Wales
- Courts do refuse recognition where justified — for example in *Aberdeenshire Council v SF* and *Argyll and Bute Council v RF*, where the adult had not been heard in the original foreign proceedings (those proceedings were in Scotland)

The process for applying for recognition and/or enforcement of foreign orders

A Schedule 3 application is to be made in accordance with Part 9 of the Court of Protection Rules 2017 and supported by Court of Protection Practice Direction 23A[41]. A copy of the Practice Direction can be found at Appendix 2.

41 https://www.judiciary.uk/guidance-and-resources/court-of-protection-practice-directions/

The application is made using form COP1 and COP24[42], together with the £421 application fee (normally via HMCTS Payment by Account (PBA). The application should be sent by post to:

Court of Protection
First Avenue House
42-49 High Holborn
London
WC1V 6NP

Form COP24 is a witness statement and should include the following:

(a) Where the application is made under rule 23.4 of the Court of Protection Rules 2017 for recognition and / or enforcement of a protective measure under paragraphs 20 or 22 of Schedule 3 to the Act:

a. Evidence to demonstrate the basis upon which it is said that the person to whom the application relates is an adult for the purposes of Schedule 3 to the Act;

b. An officially authenticated copy (and where necessary a certified translation) of the relevant court order or other document embodying the protective measure in respect of which recognition and / or enforcement is sought;

c. Confirmation that the protective measure was taken on the basis that the adult was habitually resident in the other jurisdiction;

d. Evidence to enable the Court of Protection to be satisfied—

---

[42] https://www.gov.uk/government/collections/court-of-protection-forms

(i) that the case in which the measure was taken was urgent; alternatively

(ii) that the adult to whom the protective measure related was given an opportunity to be heard by the foreign court or other body that took the protective measure.

e. Evidence to enable the court to be satisfied that the steps leading to the protective measure being made complied with any relevant provisions of the European Convention on Human Rights.

f. Details of any previous measures relating to the adult which have been the subject of a previous Schedule 3 application (whether or not such application was successful).

g. Where enforcement is sought of a protective measure that has already been recognised by the Court of Protection, a copy of the order giving effect to that recognition.

(b) Where the application is made under rule 23.5 of the Court of Protection Rules to disapply or modify a lasting power under Schedule 3 to the Act or under rule 23.6 of the Court of Protection Rules 2017 for declarations as to the authority of the donee of a lasting power, a certified copy of the lasting power (and where necessary a certified translation thereof).

Once the application has been issued a judge will give directions, including whether to join the incapacitated adult to the proceedings. An application for recognition and/or enforcement should be dealt with quickly and may be determined on the papers alone, with no hearing required. A hearing will usually be required where the application is for recognition/enforcement of a protective measure which:

(1) purports to authorise a deprivation of liberty of the adult to which it relates (other than a temporary or transient deprivation of liberty associated with the transfer of the adult to or from a specified place); or

(2) purports to authorise medical treatment.

SUMMARY

1. Confirm the foreign order is capable of recognition/enforcement

☐ Is it a protective measure within paragraph 5 (e.g., guardianship, placement, property control)?

☐ Was it made concerning an adult as defined in paragraph 4?

☐ Was it made on the basis of habitual residence in the foreign state?

☐ Does it require recognition only, enforcement, or both?

2. Prepare the Application (Part 9 CoPR and Practice Direction 23A)

Forms:

☐ COP1 (application)

☐ COP24 (witness statement – key document)

☐ Attach all required evidence (see below)

3. Evidence required in the COP24

☐ Authenticated copy of the foreign order (and translation if needed)

☐ Evidence confirming P's habitual residence in that foreign state at the date of the order

☐ Evidence that the case was urgent, or that P was given an opportunity to be heard

☐ Evidence addressing ECHR safeguards (including Article 5 if deprivation of liberty involved)

☐ Details of any previous Schedule 3 applications

☐ Evidence of compliance with foreign procedural steps

☐ If seeking enforcement of a previously recognised order → attach earlier recognition order

4. Check for obstacles to recognition (paragraphs 19(3)–(5))

☐ Was P heard (or given opportunity)? If not urgent, absence may defeat recognition

☐ Would recognition be manifestly contrary to public policy?

☐ Does the order conflict with a mandatory provision of English law?

☐ Is there a later inconsistent English measure?

5. Article 5 ECHR – if the measure involves a deprivation of liberty

☐ Has objective medical evidence justified confinement?

☐ Does P have a right to challenge the detention abroad?

☐ Is there regular review of the detention?

☐ Are safeguards "practical and effective", not theoretical?

6. Filing the Application

☐ File COP1 and COP24 with the Court of Protection (with the fee of £421) by post to Court of Protection, First Avenue House, 42-49 High Holborn, London WC1V 6NP

☐ Ask for declaration of recognition (paragraph 20)

☐ And/or declaration of enforceability (paragraph 22)

7. After filing

☐ Judicial consideration of the application

☐ A hearing may be required (usually mandatory if deprivation of liberty or medical treatment involved)

☐ If recognised and enforceable, the foreign order has effect as if it were an English order

CHAPTER THREE

PRIVATE MANDATES

Private Mandates

Article 15 of the Convention contains specific provision in relation to "powers of representation" granted by an adult "to be exercised when such adult is not in a position to protect his or her interests".

Article 15

(1) The existence, extent, modification and extinction of powers of representation granted by an adult, either under an agreement or by a unilateral act, to be exercised when such adult is not in a position to protect his or her interests, are governed by the law of the State of the adult's habitual residence at the time of the agreement or act, unless one of the laws mentioned in paragraph 2 has been designated expressly in writing.

(2) The States whose laws may be designated are –

a) State of which the adult is a national;

b) the State of a former habitual residence of the adult;

c) a State in which property of the adult is located, with respect to that property.

(3) The manner of exercise of such powers of representation is governed by the law of the State in which they are exercised.

Paragraphs 13-15 of Schedule 3 to the Mental Capacity Act 2005 incorporate similar provisions into English law:

Lasting powers of attorney, etc

13 (1) If the donor of a lasting power is habitually resident in England and Wales at the time of granting the power, the law applicable to the existence, extent, modification or extinction of the power is –

(a) the law of England and Wales, or

(b) if he specifies in writing the law of a connected country for the purpose, that law.

(2) If he is habitually resident in another country at that time, but England and Wales is a connected country, the law applicable in that respect is –

(a) the law of the other country, or

(b) if he specifies in writing the law of England and Wales for the purpose, that law.

(3) A country is connected, in relation to the donor, if it is a country –

(a) of which he is a national,

(b) in which he was habitually resident, or

(c) in which he has property.

(4) Where this paragraph applies as a result of sub-paragraph (3)(c), it applies only in relation to the property which the donor has in the connected country.

(5) The law applicable to the manner of the exercise of a lasting power is the law of the country where it is exercised.

(6) In this Part of this Schedule, 'lasting power' means –

(a) a lasting power of attorney (see section 9)

(b) an enduring power of attorney within the meaning of Schedule 4, or

(c) any other power of like effect.

A private mandate – a power of attorney would usually be considered to be a private mandate – is generally not considered to be a measure of protection and as such, the terms of the Convention in relation to recognition and enforcement do not apply (see *Re Various applications concerning foreign representative powers*[43] paragraphs 25-34 for further discussion. In this matter, it was confirmed that a power of attorney could be considered a protective measure if it been subject to a registration process *following* the mental incapacity of the donor and as such, an enduring power of attorney type document could be a protective measure. A lasting power of attorney, or similar, would not be considered a protective measure).

The general rule is that a private mandate will be governed by the law of the state of the adult's habitual residence at the time of the material agreement or act (Article 15(1) of the Convention and Paragraph 13 of Schedule 3 to the Act). There are three broad exceptions to this, which the adult must have made an express provision in writing for them to be effective:

1. the law of the state of which the adult is a national may apply;
2. the law of a former habitual residence of the adult may apply; or
3. the law of a state in which property of the adult is located may apply, with respect to that property alone.

43 [2019] EWCOP 52

Therefore:

1. If the donor was habitually resident in England and Wales at the time the power of attorney was made, it is the law of England and Wales which will apply *unless* the donor specified in writing that the law of a connected country would apply.

2. If the donor was not habitually resident in England and Wales at the time the power of attorney was made but England and Wales was a connected country, the law of the other country will apply *unless* the donor specified in writing that the law of England and Wales would apply.

A connected country is one:

- of which the donor is a national

- in which the donor is habitually resident or

- in which the donor has property.

Example

- A is domiciled in Singapore but has been living in England for the last 10 years

- They made a power of attorney in Singapore

- They have now lost capacity to manage their affairs

- The law on the creation, scope and revocation is based on the law where A was habitually resident when they made the power of attorney:

- if they were habitually resident in Singapore when it was made, the law of Singapore will apply unless they expressly stated that the law of England and Wales is to apply
- if they were habitually resident in England and Wales when they made it, the law of England and Wales will apply unless they expressly stated that the law of Singapore is to apply

Whilst the Act does not require a lasting power of attorney to expressly state which law is to apply to the existence, extent, modification and extinction, there can be issues on registration of the lasting power of attorney with the Office of the Public Guardian and as such, it is best practice to expressly state which law is to apply. For most lasting powers of attorney, it will be the law of England and Wales.

Precedent clause regarding the applicable law

The law of [territorial jurisdiction] shall be the law applicable to the existence, extent, modification or extinction of this Lasting Power of Attorney.

No matter which law governs the existence, extent, modification and extinction of the powers in question, it is the law of the state in which it is exercised which applies (see *Re Various applications concerning foreign representative powers*[44]).

The effect of Article 15(1) should be that private mandates are accepted as valid in all contracting states providing it was validly created in

[44] [2019] EWCOP 52

accordance with the law of the habitual residence of the adult (subject to Article 15(2)). In practice, however, there are likely to be issues with this.

Article 16 of the Convention and Paragraph 14 of Schedule 3 provide an additional safeguard where the exercise of a foreign power is considered to be insufficiently protective:

Article 16

Where powers of representation referred to in Article 15 are not exercised in a manner sufficient to guarantee the protection of the person or property of the adult, they may be withdrawn or modified by measures taken by an authority having jurisdiction under the Convention. Where such powers of representation are withdrawn or modified, the law referred to in Article 15 should be taken into consideration to the extent possible.

14 (1) Where a lasting power is not exercised in a manner sufficient to guarantee the protection of the person or property of the donor, the court, in exercising jurisdiction under this Schedule, may disapply or modify the power.

Where, in accordance with this Part of this Schedule, the law applicable to the power is, in one or more respects, that of a country other England and Wales, the court must, so far as possible, have regard to the law of the other country in that respect (or those respects.)

14 (1) Where a lasting power is not exercised in a manner sufficient to guarantee the protection of the person or property of the donor, the court, in exercising jurisdiction under this Schedule, may disapply or modify the power.

(2) Where, in accordance with this Part of this Schedule, the law applicable to the power is, in one or more respects, that of a country other England and Wales, the court must, so far as possible, have regard to the law of the other country in that respect (or those respects.)

The interplay between subparagraphs 14(1) and (2) is not clear but in *Re Various applications concerning foreign representative powers*[45] Senior Judge Hilder stated that they must together be interpreted as meaning that the court may disapply or modify a power so as to provide for its *exercise* in England and Wales to be no wider than the restrictions in the laws of England and Wales; and, in considering whether to disapply or modify the power, the court must have regard to the applicable law of the other state only to that extent.

Example

- A made a power of attorney in Singapore
- A has assets in England and Wales
- Under the Singaporean Mental Capacity Act 2008, there is no restriction on the making of gifts
- Section 12 of the Act places limitations on the authority of attorneys to make gifts
- The Court of Protection could make a declaration pursuant to section 15(1)(c) of the Act that the attorneys would be acting lawfully under the power of attorney, subject to

45 [2019] EWCOP 52

modifications that the authority in relation to gifts is limited to section 12 of the Act

Paragraphs 17 and 18 of Schedule 3 provide provision for the court to avoid having to give effect to the foreign power of attorney.

Mandatory rules

17 Where the court is entitled to exercise jurisdiction under this Schedule, the mandatory provisions of the law of England and Wales apply, regardless of any system of law which would otherwise apply in relation to the matter.

Public policy

18. Nothing in this Part of this Schedule requires or enables the application in England and Wales of a provision of the law in another country it is applications would be manifestly contrary to public policy.

Article 38 does provide for a partial solution which is the issue of a certificate by the authorities of a contracting state where a private mandate has been confirmed. This is replicated in paragraph 15 to Schedule 3 (but has not yet been implemented). Such a certificate would, however, only be proof of the powers stated in it at the date of the certificate.

Applications in relation to lasting powers

The Court of Protection Rules 23.5 and 23.6 deal with applications in relation to powers of attorney.

23.5 Applications in relation to lasting powers – disapplication or modification

An application under paragraph 14(1) of Schedule 3 to the Act for the court to disapply or modify a lasting power is to be made in accordance with Part 9 and any practice direction made under rule 23.1(2).

23.6 Applications in relation to lasting powers – declaration as to authority of donee of lasting power

An application for a declaration under section 15(1)(c) of the Act that a donee of a lasting power is acting lawfully when exercising authority under that lasting power is to be made in accordance with Part 9 and any practice direction made under rule 23.1(2).

Where an adult holds property in England and Wales which is likely to require ongoing management, there are various options open to the holder of a foreign power of representation.

1. The holder may seek to rely on the power, using it directly to demonstrate their authority. See https://data.parliament.uk/DepositedPapers/Files/DEP2023-0164/Letter_to_Patrick_Grady_MP_on_LPA_PMB.pdf in relation to the recognition of Scottish powers of attorney.

2. The holder may obtain an order from the country where the donor is habitually resident permitting him to manage the donor's property (essentially the equivalent of a deputyship order) and then seek recognition of that under Schedule 3.

3. The holder may seek a declaration under section 15(1)(c) and Rule 23.5 that he will be acting lawfully when exercising authority under the power in England and Wales.

In order to grant a declaration (option 3), the court would need to determine the following in accordance with paragraph 13 of Schedule 3:

(a) which law governed the existence, extent, modification or extinction of the power;

(b) whether the creation of the power met the requirements of that law;

(c) what (if any) restrictions are placed by the foreign law on the holder's powers or their exercise.

Evidence of the foreign law would need to be filed.

If a declaration were to be made, it should make clear and express the requirement that the exercise of the power in England and Wales must comply with the law of England and Wales.

The procedure for making the application is as that set out in Part 9 of the Court of Protection Rules 2017 and Practice Direction 23A and requires the filing of COP1 and COP24. A COP3 is only required if the application is asking the court to make additional declarations under sections 15 and/or 16 of the Act. The application must be accompanied by payment of the £421 application fee (normally via HMCTS Payment by Account (PBA) and sent by post to:

Court of Protection
First Avenue House
42-49 High Holborn
London
WC1V 6NP

See chapter "The process for applying for recognition and/or enforcement of foreign orders" for more detail.

SUMMARY

- A private mandate (such as a power of attorney) is not normally considered to be a protective measure, and therefore the Convention's rules on recognition/enforcement do not apply
- A private mandate is usually governed by the law of the adult's habitual residence at the time it was created, unless the adult expressly chooses another permitted law (nationality, former habitual residence, or location of property)
- The manner of exercising the mandate is governed by the law of the place where it is used (lex loci actus)
- If the mandate is not being used properly, authorities with jurisdiction may withdraw or modify it to protect the adult (Convention Article 16; Schedule 3, paragraph 14)
- Courts in England and Wales must still apply mandatory English law and may refuse to apply foreign law if it is contrary to public policy
- To use a foreign power in England and Wales, the holder may:
    - rely on the power directly,
    - obtain a foreign protective order and seek recognition under Schedule 3, or

   - apply for a declaration confirming they are acting lawfully under the power.

- When seeking such a declaration, the court must determine:
   - which law governs the power,
   - whether it was validly created, and
   - what restrictions that foreign law imposes and whether its operation should be limited

CHAPTER FOUR

ALTERNATIVE OPTIONS

Alternative option: application to appoint a deputy (section 16 of the Act)

An alternative to applying to the Court of Protection for recognition and/or enforcement of an order made outside of England and Wales or for the use of a private mandate is for an application to be made pursuant to sections 16-18 of the Act to appoint a deputy. The Court of Protection will have jurisdiction to do this if one of the requirements of paragraph 7 of Schedule 3 to the Act are satisfied (an adult habitually resident in England and Wales, an adult's property in England and Wales, and adult present in England and Wales or who has property there if the matter is urgent, or an adult present in England and Wales if it is a protective measure which is temporary and limited in relation to him). If the person has assets in England and Wales but is not habitually resident there, the Court of Protection will only have jurisdiction in relation to the incapacitated person's property and financial affairs, not their personal welfare.

A deputy is appointed to act in a fiduciary capacity on behalf of the incapacitated person in relation to their property and financial affairs and/or personal welfare (depending on the terms of the order). A deputy has stringent regulatory and reporting requirements.

SUMMARY

- Instead of applying for recognition/enforcement of a foreign order or a private mandate, an applicant may seek to appoint a deputy under sections 16–18 of the Act
- The Court of Protection can only appoint a deputy if one of the jurisdiction grounds in paragraph 7 of Schedule 3 to the Act is met (e.g., habitual residence or property in England and Wales)
- If the adult has property in England and Wales but is not habitually resident there, the court's jurisdiction is limited to property and financial affairs, not personal welfare
- A deputy (property and affairs or personal welfare) acts in a fiduciary capacity, making decisions on behalf of the adult and complying with strict supervision and reporting requirements
- The appointment of a deputy (potentially time limited) may be used as a practical workaround when a foreign order cannot easily be recognised or enforced under Schedule 3

The application process to appoint a deputy

An application to appoint a deputy is begun in the same way as any other first application to the Court of Protection; in accordance with Part 9 of the Court of Protection Rules 2017. Applications relating to property and affairs are supplemented by Practice Direction 9H (Property and Affairs Deputyship Applications) [46]. A copy is attached at Appendix 3.

Application forms are available online via the HMCTS website: www.gov.uk/government/collections/court-of-protection-forms.

For a first application, the following documents must be lodged:

- COP1 – application form (there is a digitalised version of this when the application is filed online);

- COP1A (property and affairs) *or* COP1B (welfare) – supporting information form;

- COP2 – permission application (only required for welfare deputyship applications where permission has not already been granted);

- COP3 – assessment of capacity;

- COP4 – deputy's declaration;

- any other supporting evidence (to be included in a COP24); and

- payment of the £421 application fee (normally via HMCTS Payment by Account (PBA), unless already paid on an application for permission).

Before the application is made, it is necessary for P to be personally notified of the application. The process for this is set out in Practice

46 https://www.judiciary.uk/guidance-and-resources/court-of-protection-practice-directions/

Direction 7A and is done using form COP14PADep which provides the following information:

(a) who the applicant is;

(b) that the application raises the question of whether P lacks capacity in relation to a matter or matters and what that means;

(c) what will happen if the Court makes an order or direction that has been applied for;

(d) details of the person it is proposed should be appointed to make decisions on behalf of P in relation to their property and affairs;

(e) that P may seek advice and assistance in relation to the application;

(f) that P may complete and return the form to the person notifying them to acknowledge notification and indicate their wishes and feelings about the application;

(g) that the notification form must be returned to the applicant before the end of 14 days from the date P received it, and if it is not sent within this period, the Court will assume that P does not object;

(h) that P may, in addition to sending the completed form back to the applicant, send a copy of it to the Court; and

(i) that at the point the application is made, the applicant will be required to provide to the Court a copy of the notification form if it has been completed and returned to the applicant.

The COP14PADep also contains a section to be completed by the person who personally notifies P to record the steps taken to explain the application to P, the extent to which they understood or appeared to understand and any response they gave and any wishes and feelings P expressed about the application.

It is considered to be a principle of natural justice and although the Court of Protection can dispense with notice (Rule 6.10 Court of Protection Rules 2017), it is unlikely to do. The decision to dispense with service is not a decision made by reference to P's best interests. Case law suggests that the court is highly unlikely to agree to the dispense of service on either the donor or a notifiable person (see for example *Re AB*[47], *I v D*[48], *Re P (Statutory Will)*[49] and *Re P (Statutory Will) (Costs Application)*[50] where a costs order was made against the applicant). In *DXL v PXL*[51] it was reiterated that establishing the views of a person lacking capacity are still relevant if he or she lacks capacity to make the decision in question (which accords with the UN Convention on the Rights of Persons with Disabilities, in particular Article 3). As such, a person in the claimant's position should be informed of the details of a settlement award because this would be to treat him in the same way as a person without a disability and to not do so, would 'constitute an interference with basic rights' as well as 'a serious interference with common law rights' and Article 8 of the ECHR rights.

It is also necessary to notify various third parties of the application. This is done in accordance with Practice Direction 9B and is done using form COP15PADep which provides the following information:

---

47 [2014] COPLR 381

48 [2016] COPLR 432

49 [2024] EWCOP 12

50 [2024] EWCOP 9

51 [2019] EWHC 2579 (QB)

(i) who the applicant is;

(ii) details about the person to whom the application relates (P);

(iii) details of the application being made and the order or orders sought;

(iv) the full name and address of the person being notified and their connection to P;

(v) that the person notified is asked to complete the form and return it to the application no more than 14 days after receiving it, to acknowledge notification and to indicate whether they consent or object to the application;

(vi) that the person may, in addition to sending the completed form back to the applicant, send a copy of it to the Court; and

(vii) that at the point an application is made, the applicant is required to provide to the Court all completed notification forms where these have been returned to the application within the prescribed time.

As with notification of P, the Court of Protection can authorise the dispensation of service but it is unlikely to do so. *United Lincolnshire Hospitals NHS Trust v CD*[52] was an example of where notice was dispensed with on the basis that having taken '*all the circumstances of [the] matter into consideration, and firmly on the basis that X's interests will not be materially or adversely affected by the substantive application, [HHJ Hilder] was satisfied that it is appropriate to dispense with any requirement to notify X of [the] proceedings (or serve him with the application papers)*'. It seems from the judgment that HHJ Hilder may not have reached the same conclusion had X been materially or adversely affected by the

52 [2019] EWCOP 24

application. Furthermore, in other circumstances (principally because of the extreme nature of his behaviour and 'unlawful actions'), HHJ Hilder may have still determined that in the interests of procedural fairness, X should not have been excluded from the proceedings even if he was not likely to be materially or adversely affected by the application.

Court of Protection Practice Direction 9B sets out the mandatory categories. At least three persons must be notified, and all persons in a class must be notified, even if this exceeds three.

Mandatory classes include:

- spouse/civil partner
- cohabiting partner
- parents/guardians
- children
- siblings
- grandparents/grandchildren
- aunts/uncles
- nieces/nephews
- step-parents
- half-siblings

If fewer than three exist, the applicant should consider notifying:

- close friends

- GP or consultant
- care home manager

The applicant must not file the application until either:

1. acknowledgements of notification have been received from all required recipients; or
2. 14 days have passed since the latest notification to P or any person required to be notified.

One of the most common reasons for rejection of deputy applications is that insufficient persons have been notified.

If more than three months pass from the first notification without the application being filed, fresh notification must be given.

Applications should be made via the Court of Protection's online portal. The applicant must:

1. complete the online form, signing the statement of truth and acknowledging that the Court may contact any persons notified;
2. provide details of:
    - the date P was notified and steps taken to assist P's understanding;
    - P's wishes and feelings regarding the application;
    - the persons notified and their relationship to P;
    - the dates of notification or reasons why notification was not possible;

    - whether each notified person consents, objects, or has not responded;

3. upload all notification acknowledgements and all supporting documents required under rule 9.4 and Practice Direction 9A; and

4. pay the application fee (professional users should use PBA where possible).

If the applicant instead files a paper application (which the Court may refuse), they must lodge:

- a signed COP1 with a statement of truth and full notification details;

- COP14PADep recording notification to P, steps taken to support understanding, and P's wishes and feelings;

- all returned notification acknowledgements;

- all supporting documents required by rule 9.4 and Practice Direction 9A; and

- the application fee.

Property and affairs deputyship applications must now be made through the online system. Health and welfare deputyship applications remain paper-based. The updated (December 2024) Practice Direction 9H confirms that professional applicants may be refused their costs if they fail to use the online portal for property and affairs deputyship applications (new or replacement).

Once the order has been made, if an amendment needs to be made it should be done using form COP9 (with a COP24 if necessary) within

21 days of the order with the words "CORRECTION REQUEST" being added to the first page.

The COP3, Assessment of Capacity form, should be completed by a professional medical practitioner, such as a GP, Psychiatrist or Mental Health Professional. If there is any doubt about P's capacity or there is any prospect of an objection being raised to the application, the COP3 should be completed by a specialist psychiatrist, psycho-geriatrician or similarly other qualified consultant experienced in assessing cognitive impairment and mental capacity. If there is any doubt about P's capacity and the COP3 has been completed by a General Practitioner or Health professional, and a subsequent objection is raised, it is likely that the Court will require a Specialist Capacity Assessment to be carried out and as such, it is preferable to submit this at the outset.

Theis J has confirmed in *CT v London Borough of Lambeth & Anor* [2025] EWCOP 6 (T3) the following checklist for those assessing capacity:

> *(1) The first three statutory principles in s 1 MCA 2005 must be applied in a non-discriminatory manner to ensure those with mental impairments are not deprived of their equal right to make decisions where they can be supported to do so.*
>
> *(2) In respect of the third principle regarding unwise decisions, particular care must be taken to avoid the protection imperative and the risk of pathologising disagreements.*
>
> *(3) As set out in A Local Authority v JB [2021] UKSC 52, whether the person is able to make the decisions must first be addressed. Only if it is proven that one or more of the statutory criteria are not satisfied should the assessor them proceed to consider whether such inability is because of a mental impairment.*
>
> *(4) Those assessing capacity must vigilantly ensure that the assessment is evidence-based, person-centred, criteria-focussed and non-*

judgmental, and not made to depend, implicitly or explicitly, upon the identification of a so-called unwise outcome.

(5) *Insight is a clinical concept, whereas decision making capacity is a legal concept. Capacity assessors must be aware of the conceptual distinction and that, depending on the evidence, a person may be able to make a particular decision even if they are described as lacking insight into their general condition.*

(6) *In some cases, a lack of insight may be relevant to, but not determinative of, whether the person has a mental impairment for the purposes of s2 MCA 2005.*

(7) *When assessing and determining the legal test for mental capacity, all that is required is the application of the statutory words in ss2-3 MCA 2005 without any gloss; having 'insight' into mental impairment is not part of that test.*

(8) *Relevant information will be different in each case but will include the nature of the decisions, the reason why the decision is needed, and the likely effects of deciding one way or another, or making no decision at all.*

(9) *The relevant information is to be shared with the individual and the individual should be supported to understand the relevant information. The individual is not required to identify relevant information him/herself.*

(10) *If a lack of insight is considered to be relevant to the assessment of capacity, the assessor must clearly record what they mean by a lack of insight in this context and how they believe it affects, or does not affect, the person's ability to make the decision as defined by the statutory criteria, for example to use/weigh relevant information.*

Applications for the appointment of a personal welfare deputy are rare (see *Re Lawson, Mottram and Hopton (appointment of personal welfare deputies)*[53] and *Parr v Cheshire East Council & Anor*[54] which did permit the appointment of a personal welfare deputy but it was distinguished from the *Lawson* judgment). As such, an application for recognition and enforcement of a personal welfare order may be preferred.

SUMMARY

1. Confirm you are making the correct type of application

☐ Are you applying for a deputyship under the MCA 2005 (property and affairs or welfare)?

☐ Is the application being made using the correct COP forms (COP1, COP1A/COP1B, COP2 if needed)?

☐ Has P's capacity been evidenced in a COP3?

☐ Has the proposed deputy completed COP4?

2. Prepare the Application (Part 9 CoPR Rules and PD 9H)

Forms to lodge:

☐ COP1 – application form (digital version if using online portal)

53 [2019] EWCOP 22

54 [2026] EWCOP 1 (T3)

☐ COP1A (property) or COP1B (welfare) – supporting information

☐ COP2 – permission (only if required for welfare applications)

☐ COP3 – capacity assessment (preferably by a specialist if any doubt)

☐ COP4 – deputy declaration

☐ COP24 – any additional evidence or witness statement

☐ £421 fee (via PBA where possible)

3. Notification Requirements (Natural Justice Principles)

☐ Notify P using COP14PADep, explaining the application, proposed deputy, and P's rights

☐ Ensure P is given 14 days to respond; if no reply, court assumes no objection

☐ Record steps taken to support P's understanding and any wishes/feelings expressed

☐ Notify at least three mandatory categories of relatives using COP15PADep

☐ Provide notified persons with 14 days to respond (consent/objection/no reply)

☐ Ensure ALL persons in a relevant class are notified (even if more than three)

☐ Notify substitutes (e.g., close friends, GP, care home manager) if fewer than three exist

☐ Do not file until:

- all acknowledgements received or
- 14 days have passed since the last notification

☐ Fresh notification required if application not filed within 3 months

4. Filing the Application

☐ Complete online form with full notification details, dates, relationships, and responses

☐ Upload all COP14PADep and COP15PADep acknowledgements

☐ Upload all supporting documents required under Rule 9.4 and PD 9A

☐ Pay the application fee

☐ Property and affairs deputyships must be filed online (PD 9H)

☐ Welfare deputyships currently remain paper-based

5. Supporting Evidence and Good Practice

☐ Ensure COP3 is completed by a suitably qualified professional (specialist if any doubt)

☐ Anticipate objections—submit a high-quality COP3 at the outset

☐ Welfare deputyships are rare; consider whether the application meets criteria (*Re Lawson, Mottram and Hopton*)

Alternative option: application for a one-off order (section 16 of the Act)

Section 16 of the Act permits the court to make a one-off order, which may be more appropriate where a single decision (such as access to a bank account) is required. This approach would be most consistent with section 1 of the Act and in particular, section 1(6) which states:

> *(6) Before the act is done, or the decision is made, regard must be had to whether the purpose for which it is needed can be as effectively achieved in a way that is less restrictive of the person's rights and freedom of action.*

The application process is similar to that for appointing a deputy (the digital application process is not currently available) and requires filing of:

- COP1
- COP1A
- COP3

- COP24
- payment of the £421 application fee (normally via HMCTS Payment by Account (PBA), unless already paid on an application for permission).

The application should be sent by post to:

Court of Protection
First Avenue House
42-49 High Holborn
London
WC1V 6NP

Once the application has been issued, the incapacitated person and those identified to be notified will need to be notified using forms COP14 and COP15 in accordance with:

1. Court of Protection practice direction 7A (notifying P) which sets out the process for notifying P. Such notice must be provided to the incapacitated trustee personally (Rule 7.8 Court of Protection Rules 2017).

    - P must be notified:

        (a) that an application form has been issued by the court or withdrawn;

        (b) that an appellant's notice has been issued by the court or withdrawn;

        (c) that the court has made a decision relating to him or her (other than a case management decision);

(d) of a direction under rule 1.2 and of the appointment of a litigation friend, accredited legal representative, or representative on his or her behalf;

(e) of any other matter as the court may direct.

- The practice direction sets out the information to be included in the form COP14 (notification form) being:

    (a) who the applicant is;

    (b) what the application is about;

    (c) what will happen if the court makes the order or direction that has been applied for; and

    (d) that P may seek advice and assistance in relation to any matter of which P is notified.

2. Court of Protection practice direction 9B (notification of other persons that an application form has been issued) which sets out who should be notified and the method of notification. Further detail about this can be found in the section relating to the appointment of a deputy.

Following notification, forms COP20A and COP20B must be returned to the Court of Protection within 7 days of notification (Rules 7.10 and 6.8 Court of Protection Rules 2017). As mentioned above, it is highly unlikely that the court will authorise notification of P or a notifiable person to be dispensed with.

CHAPTER FIVE

WHERE P HAS ASSETS ABROAD OR MOVES ABROAD

Where P has assets abroad and has an existing deputy or attorney

Practitioners should not be advising on the law of the country where P has moved or holds assets, unless they are qualified to do so. A suitable adviser may be identified at https://www.step.org/directory/members.

Where P has assets in the foreign country and/or a decision needs to be made, it is likely the country in which the asset is situated/where the decision needs to be made will have jurisdiction. Generally speaking, the deputy or attorney will have four options:

1. the third party in the country where the asset is situated/decision is to be made may accept the Court of Protection order or power of attorney without any further authority;

2. the third party may accept a specific order of the Court of Protection authorising the authorised person to deal with the assets in the foreign jurisdiction (a precedent order can be found at Appendix 6);

3. the third party may require an application to a court in that country for the Court of Protection order to be recognised and/or enforced (notwithstanding an order being granted, consider authority (including authority for costs) being separately granted by the Court of Protection);

4. the third party may require the appointment of a deputy equivalent/decision maker in the country in which the asset is

situated/decision to be made (again, consider the issue of the authority to do this and to incur costs).

It is suggested that the first step is to provide a copy of the Court of Protection order or power of attorney to the third party and to ask what their requirements are for being able to deal with the asset/make the decision.

A deputyship order made in England and Wales is likely to give the deputy authority to make decisions about P's assets, wherever situated. However, if the deputy is required to take steps to have the order recognised/enforced or apply for a form of deputyship order or one off order in that country, this may be considered beyond a deputy's standard authority (*ACC & Ors (property and affairs deputy; recovering assets costs for legal proceedings)*[55]). As such, it is advisable for express authority to be issued by the Court of Protection for the deputy to deal with P's assets abroad and for them to be able to charge P's estate for doing so. An example order for this can be found at Appendix 7.

Authority in relation to powers of attorney has not been tested but the principles of *Re ACC* should be considered, with specific authority being obtained from the Court of Protection if appropriate.

Scotland

With regard to Scotland, the Law Society has produced guidance (https://www.lawsociety.org.uk/topics/private-client/cross-border-mental-capacity-frameworks) setting out the relevant legal frameworks in England and Wales and Scotland in relation to powers of attorney. Paragraph 3.3 states that the sheriff in *An Application by C re E,* Airdrie Sheriff Court, 2 April 2013 (unreported) held that a properly registered English EPA had automatic effect in Scotland. However, in practice third party organisations (usually financial organisations) will require some

55 [2020] EWCOP 9

form of Scottish endorsement. Whilst there is no provision in the Adults with Incapacity (Scotland) Act 2000 for having a non-Scottish power of attorney formally endorsed, the Scottish OPG has created a certificate which can be printed and presented with the power of attorney. A copy of the certificate can be found at https://www.publicguardian-scotland.gov.uk/docs/librariesprovider3/poa/pdf-documents/certificate.pdf?sfvrsn=12.

P moving abroad

A deputyship order continues unless and until the deputy is discharged or P dies. Where P moves abroad and has an existing deputy appointed in England and Wales, it may be appropriate for the appointment to continue (providing the Court of Protection retains jurisdiction, most likely on the basis that P has assets in England and Wales).

With regard to concurrent jurisdiction, the doctrine of *forum non conveniens* applies (which country is most convenient): *JO v GO & Ors*[56]. A decision to refuse to exercise jurisdiction on this basis is not a best interests decision.

Depending on P's circumstances, it may no longer be necessary for a deputy to remain appointed in England and Wales. The Court of Protection would have to be satisfied that it was in P's best interests for their assets to be transferred to the control of a deputy equivalent in another jurisdiction. If an application is to be made, it is necessary to include information about the appointed deputy equivalent and what arrangements there are in place to supervise the deputy equivalent and safeguard P and their estate. An example order authorising a transfer of assets to another jurisdiction and discharging the English deputy can be found at Appendix 7.

56 [2013] EWHC 3932 (COP)

See the judgment of Senior Judge Hilder in *Potter Rees Dolan Trust Corporation Limited v WL*[57] where it was determined to be in ML's best interests for the English deputy to remain, notwithstanding that he had returned to Poland, was considered to be habitually resident there and there was a deputyship type system in place in Poland.

As mentioned previously, in *Irwin Mitchell Trust Corporation v KS & Ors*[58] the Court of Protection retained jurisdiction in relation to a minor who had moved to India in relation to the assets held in England.

Whilst not strictly within the parameters of this book but as it may be of use to practitioners, it is worth mentioning the checklist contained in *Re UR*[59] which practitioners and the Court of Protection should consider when it is being asked to consider whether a person should leave the country permanently:

"

i. *Liaison with the relevant Embassy/ Consulate (in the first instance) to ascertain what guidance and assistance can be provided;*

ii. *Evidence as to physical health to travel (GP);*

iii. *Evidence as to mental health to travel (psychiatrist);*

iv. *Legal opinion regarding citizenship, benefit entitlement, health and social care provision in the relevant country, and such other issues relevant to the case;*

---

57 [2023] EWCOP 19

58 [2025] EWCOP 7

59 [2021] EWCOP 10

v. *Consideration of any applications that need to be made as a consequence of any legal opinion provided;*

vi. *Independent social work evidence regarding the viability of the proposed package of care in the relevant country if such evidence cannot be provided by the parties to the proceedings or a direction under section 49 MCA;*

vii. *Confirmation of travel costings from the commissioners of the care package, both in relation to P and any carers that may need to travel with them (who will pay?);*

viii. *Confirmation that the necessary medication/ care will be available during travel from the UK/ for the immediate future in the new country;*

ix. *Transition plan/ care plan, to include a contingency plan and how the matter should return to court in the event of an emergency in implementing the proposed plan;*

x. *Best interest evidence from the relevant commissioners;*

xi. *Wishes and feelings evidence;*

xii. *Residual orders to allow the plan to be implemented, including single issue financial orders regarding opening/closing of UK bank accounts, the purchasing of essential items to travel (if necessary);*

xiii. *Covid-19 considerations prior to travel (if applicable)"*

If the Court of Protection makes a personal welfare order to the effect it is in P's best interests to move abroad, the court will only retain jurisdiction in relation to personal welfare if P remains habitually resident in England and Wales and so any decisions required by the Court of

Protection, should be sought before any possible change of habitual residence.

A copy of the order made in *Re UR* (as included in the judgment) can be found at Appendix 8.

SUMMARY

- Practitioners must not advise on foreign law unless qualified to do so
- If P has foreign assets or decisions to be made abroad, that country usually has jurisdiction although the Court of Protection may also retain jurisdiction
- Foreign third parties may: accept the COP order; require a specific COP order; require recognition by their own court; or require a local deputy equivalent
- An English power of attorney (LPA or EPA) should be usable in Scotland without express endorsement. Best practice suggests adding a certificate https://www.publicguardian-scotland.gov.uk/docs/librariesprovider3/poa/pdf-documents/certificate.pdf?sfvrsn=12.

CHAPTER SIX

CASE STUDIES

Case study 1

John, a man in his 60s living with dementia has been residing in Spain for 20 years with his wife, Mavis. He has been removed to England and Wales by his son, Eric, due to safeguarding concerns. John has no capacity to consent to the move. John has no assets in England and Wales. Eric applies to the Court of Protection for an order determining it is in John's best interests to remain in a care home in England.

Would the situation be different if John had assets in England and Wales and Eric was seeking an order in relation to John's property and affairs?

Based on *Re QD (Jurisdiction: Habitual Residence) (No 1).*

Issues to consider:

- Does the Court of Protection have jurisdiction?
    - Capacity – sections 2 and 3 and paragraph 4 of schedule 3 MCA 2005
    - Schedule 3 to the MCA 2005
    - Habitual residence
    - Property in England and Wales
    - Present in England and Wales, if the matter is urgent

  - Present in England and Wales, if a protective measure is temporary and limited in its effect to England and Wales

  - Urgency – only justified where substantive orders are necessary in order to avert an immediate threat to life or safety or where there in an immediate need for further or other protection (*Re QD*)

- Habitual residence

  - Treated as habitually resident if habitual residence cannot be ascertained, he is a refugee or he has been displaced as a result of disturbance in the country of his habitual residence (paragraph 7(2) of schedule 3)

  - Question of fact – has there been integration (*An English Local Authority v SW*)? Situation before the move? Length of time (*AB v SX*)?

- Doctrine of necessity

  - It will not apply where there is bad faith or where what is done is unreasonable or not in the best interests of the assist person (*Re MN; Re QD*)

  - Question of authority to remove is key (*Re MN*) – must be proper and lawful

  - Cannot convert what was a wrongful act into a justified act (*Re QD*)

- Inherent jurisdiction if John is not habitually resident

  - o Does the matter fall outside of the statutory scheme to which the inherent jurisdiction applies (*A Local Authority v DL*)

Court is unlikely to consider John is habitually resident in England and Wales and therefore is unlikely to have jurisdiction (unless it can be established it requires an urgent order or if a protective measure is temporary and limited in effect).

Where John has assets in England and Wales:

- The Court of Protection would have jurisdiction as John has property in England and Wales.

- If there is a Spanish protective measure in place, an application could be made for its recognition/enforcement.

- Alternatively:

  - o The Court of Protection could make a one off order under section 16 of the Act to manage Anthony's property and affairs in England and Wales

  - o Depending on the decisions required, a deputy could be appointed (potentially for a time limited order) pursuant to section 16 of the Act.

- See case study 4 for if John had made a power of attorney in Spain.

<u>Case study 2</u>

Sarah, a Scottish woman in her 40s living with a brain injury has been living in a care home in England for 7 years. Sarah has a guardian (property and affairs and personal welfare) appointed in Scotland and her parents are considering an application to the Court of Protection for recognition and enforcement of the order.

Based on *Aberdeenshire Council v SF & Ors.*

Same issues to consider as for case study 1. Need to establish habitual residence first and then consider the checklist in *Aberdeenshire Council v SF, EF and Sunderland City Council* (Appendix 1). Case law suggests that Sarah may not be habitually resident in England and Wales but even if she is, the court is unlikely to recognise or enforce the order if she was not given an opportunity to be heard in the original proceedings and there is any mechanism for reviewing any deprivation of liberty.

Case study 3

Anna, a woman in her 80s lives in New Zealand. She has made an Enduring Power of Attorney in New Zealand. Her attorney is seeking access to cash assets in the UK.

This is based on *Re Various applications concerning foreign representative powers (specifically AB 13285001).*

Issues to consider:

- Habitual residence

- Jurisdiction of the court (assets in England and Wales)

- Whether the power of attorney is to continue notwithstanding any loss of capacity

- Whether Anna has lost capacity to manage the assets

- Whether there is any provision in the country for registration or confirmation of the power (if there was, it may be considered a protective measure)

- If it is considered a private mandate (which it would be as there is no provision for registration or confirmation of the power), the options are:

    - Seek a declaration pursuant to section 15(1) of the Act that the attorney would be acting lawfully in exercise of the power of attorney in respect of Anna's property and affairs in England and Wales

    - The Court of Protection could make a one off order under section 16 of the Act to manage Anna's property and affairs in England and Wales

    - Depending on the decisions required, a deputy could be appointed (potentially for a time limited order) pursuant to section 16 of the Act.

<u>Case study 4</u>

Anthony has made a power of attorney in Spain. He has assets in England and Wales which require managing.

This is Re Various applications concerning foreign representative powers (specifically AJC 13286102).

Issues to consider:

- Habitual residence

- Jurisdiction of the court (assets in England and Wales)

- Whether the power of attorney is to continue notwithstanding any loss of capacity (in Spain, this is unlikely)

- Whether Anthony has lost capacity to manage the assets

- Whether there is any provision in the country for registration or confirmation of the power

- If the court is not able to make a declaration that the attorney(s) would be acting lawfully in exercise of the power of attorney on the basis it would not continue beyond incapacity, the options are:

    - The Spanish court could appoint a Tutor or Curador (if Anthony is resident in Spain) and an application could be made to the Court of Protection for recognition/enforcement.

    - The Court of Protection could make a one off order under section 16 of the Act to manage Anthony's property and affairs in England and Wales

    - Depending on the decisions required, a deputy could be appointed (potentially for a time limited order) pursuant to section 16 of the Act.

APPENDIX A

Checklist for cases proceeding under Part 4 of Schedule 3 to the Mental Capacity Act 2005 seeking recognition and enforcement of a foreign measure (where no previous order has been made in relation to P in England or Wales).

Basic details

Name of Protected Adult (P)	
Date of birth of P	
Foreign Court	
Name of foreign judge	
Date of foreign protective measure	
Copy of foreign order provided?	
Summary of terms of foreign measure	
Copy of foreign judgment provided?	
Does foreign measure require deprivation of P's liberty?	

Did foreign judgment address checklist?	
Date of Schedule 3 application	
Date of COP 24	
Has applicant completed checklist?	

Instructions and key to symbols:

- Answer the questions in the order that they are set out keeping in mind the General Principles below.
- The Questions are in black script.
- Instructions are in red script.
- ¶ used before a number denotes exclusively a numbered paragraph in Schedule 3.
- § used before a number denotes exclusively a numbered paragraph in an authority.
- P is the Protected Adult.
- † denotes Questions to be answered directly (see below).
- ⁋ denotes Questions where findings of fact of the foreign court are conclusive (see below).
- ‡ denotes Questions where Anglo-Welsh law applies (see below).

General principles:

- COPR PD23A para 12 contains a list of the matters to be included in, or attached to, the COP 24 witness statement accompanying the Schedule 3 application. This checklist does not derogate from that list. Rather, it is intended to complement that list to seek to ensure that all of the requirements of Schedule 3 and of the Human Rights Act 1998 are complied with.

- In answering the Questions regard may only be had to the merits of a foreign measure in order to establish whether the measure complies with the criteria in Schedule 3 (see ¶24).

- Questions 1, 2, 5, 7, 8, 9, 10, 11, 12, 20 should be answered directly without applying principles or concepts of English-Welsh law or the law of the foreign court. These Questions are marked † in the YES/NO column.

- Any finding of fact made by the foreign court is conclusive as regards Questions 9 – 12 (see ¶21). These Questions are marked ⁋ in the YES/NO column.

- Principles of English-Welsh law should be applied when answering Questions 3, 4, 6, 13, 14, 15, 16, 17, 18, 19, 22. These Questions are marked ‡ in the YES/NO column

- The answer to Q21 will be a mixture of the above.

QUESTION	Ref	ANSWER	REASON
Recognition 1. Is P under 16?	¶4(1)(b)	YES/NO †	

If yes, Schedule 3 does not apply. If no, go to Question 2.			
2. Where P is 16 or 17: is P habitually resident in a country that has adopted the 1996 Hague Convention? If yes, Schedule 3 does not apply. If no or N/A, go to Question 3.	¶4(2)(a)	YES/NO (or N/A) †	
3. Is it necessary that P is joined as a party? (Normally, necessity will be shown only where P is actively contesting the application and where there are other valid reasons to review the process of the foreign court.) If yes, go to Question 4. If no, go to Question 5.	HSE v CNWL [2015] EWCOP 48 §35	YES/NO ‡	
4. Does P have capacity to conduct the Schedule 3 litigation? (Note: this question is to be answered applying ss.2 & 3 Mental Capacity Act 2005) If yes, join P and go to Question 5. If no, join P, either appoint an Accredited Legal Representative for P under COPR r.17.1 or a litigation friend for P under COPR r.17.4, and then go to Question 5.	COPR r. 23.3(2)	YES/NO ‡	
5. Is P a person who as a result of an impairment or insufficiency of their personal faculties, cannot protect their interests?	¶4(2)(a)	YES/NO †	

If yes, go to Question 6. If no, Schedule 3 does not apply.			
6. Does P nonetheless have capacity to take the material decision(s) applying ss.2 & 3 Mental Capacity Act 2005? If yes, note that this factor must be specifically considered under Question 14. Now go to Question 7. If no, go to Question 7.	Re PA [2015] EWCOP 38, §98	YES/NO ‡	
7. Does the foreign measure provide for any of the following: a. the determination of incapacity and the institution of a protective regime b. placing P under the protection of an appropriate authority c. guardianship, curatorship or any corresponding system d. the designation and functions of a person having charge of the P's person or property, or representing or otherwise helping him e. placing P in a place where protection can be provided f. administering, conserving or disposing of P's property g. authorising a specific intervention for the protection of the person or property of P? If yes to any of these, go to Question 8.	¶5(1)	YES/NO †	

If no to all of these, the measure cannot be recognised and/or enforced.			
8. Was the foreign measure taken on the ground that P was habitually resident in that country? If yes, go to Question 9. If no, the foreign measure cannot be recognised.	¶19(1)	YES/NO †	
9. Did the foreign court find as a fact that P was habitually resident in that country as at the date of the measure?" If yes, go to Question 11. If no, go to Question 10.	¶21	YES/NO †⁋	
10. Is there is any reason to doubt that the measure was taken on the basis that the adult was at that date habitually resident in that country? If yes, adjourn the case to obtain clarification from the foreign court. Once clarified go to Question 11. If no, go to Question 11.	¶21	YES/NO †⁋	
11. Was the foreign case urgent? If yes, go to Question 14 If no, go to Question 12.	¶19(3)(a)`	YES/NO †⁋	
12. Was P given the opportunity to be heard?	¶19(3)(b)	YES/NO †⁋	

If yes, go to Question 14. If no, go to Question 13.			
13. Was the omission to give P the opportunity to be heard contrary to natural justice? If yes, the foreign measure cannot be recognised. If no go to Question 14.	¶19(3)(c)	YES/NO ‡	
14. Would recognition of this specific measure, on the facts of this specific case, be manifestly contrary to public policy? Note: if answer to Question 6 is that P has the mental capacity to make the material decisions, then P will be a capacitous albeit vulnerable adult. Very careful consideration will need to be given as to whether to recognise the foreign measure in these specific circumstances would be manifestly contrary to public policy. If yes, the foreign measure cannot be recognised. If no, go to Question 15.	¶19(4)(a)	YES/NO ‡	
15. Is the measure inconsistent with a mandatory provision of the law of England and Wales? Note that where the applicant alone is represented, the Court will need to be satisfied that sufficient material has been placed before the Court to support this answer.	¶19(4)(b)	YES/NO ‡	

If yes, the foreign measure cannot be recognised. If no, go to Q16.			
Article 5 ECHR In answering Questions 16 – 18 a light touch is to be applied 16. Does the measure provide for the compulsory placement and treatment of P, therefore amounting to a deprivation of liberty for the purposes of Article 5 of the ECHR? If yes, go to Question 17. If no, **the foreign measure is to be recognised and a declaration made to that effect**. Then go to Question 20.	Re PA, §96 HSE v EM §35	YES/NO ‡	
17. Has objective medical expertise established that P's medical disorder is of a kind and degree that warrants compulsory confinement? If yes, go to Question 18. If no, the foreign measure cannot be recognised.	ibid	YES/NO ‡	
18. Does P have the right in the foreign country to challenge the detention? If yes, go to Question 19. If no, the foreign measure cannot be recognised.	Re PA, §§96-97	YES/NO ‡	

19. Will P's detention in the foreign country be regularly reviewed? If yes, **the foreign measure is to be recognised and a declaration made to that effect**. Then go to Question 20. If no, the foreign measure cannot be recognised.	ibid	YES/NO ‡	
Enforcement 20. Has an application been made for a declaration as to whether a foreign measure is enforceable in England and Wales? If yes, go to Question 21. If no, go to Question 22.	¶22(1)	YES/NO †	
21. Is the foreign measure entitled to be recognised under Questions 16 or 18? If yes, a declaration that the foreign measure is enforceable in England and Wales **must** be made. Now go to Question 22.	¶22(2)	YES/NO †⁋ ‡	
Implementation 22. Is the Court satisfied, applying ss.1(5) and 4 MCA 2005, that implementing the order in England & Wales would not be contrary to the adult's best interests?" If yes, no further action If no, adjourn case for remedial steps	¶12 Re MN [2010] EWHC 1926 (Fam) §§31, 35	YES/NO ‡	

to be taken in accordance with directions.			
Consider *Argyll and Bute Council v RF* and *Aberdeenshire Council v SF, EF and Sunderland City Council* and *Re PQ* – was P given an opportunity to be heard in the original proceedings?			

Additional questions following *Argyll and Bute Council v RF* [2025] EWCOP 12 (T3) (15 April 2025)

Q18 (Right to challenge the detention – Art 5(4)) — add an explicit inquiry about P's representation and effective opportunity to be heard in the foreign proceedings.

Why: In RF, Theis J stressed that, where the foreign measure was not urgent, failure to join P or to provide independent representation (e.g., safeguarder/advocate) meant P was not given an effective opportunity to be heard, engaging Sch 3 para 19(3)(b)–(c) (natural justice) and rendering recognition unlawful under s.6 HRA 1998.

Q19 (Regular review of detention – Art 5(4)) — extend the question to require that any review is "practical and effective", with P represented throughout the review period.

Why: Re PQ confirms that Article 5(4) compliance requires P to have a representative (litigation friend, ALR or r.1.2 representative) throughout the currency of the authorisation where there is a court-authorised deprivation of liberty; without this, rights are "theoretical and illusory." RF picks up the same thread when deciding whether to recognise a foreign measure authorising a deprivation of liberty.

APPENDIX B

PRACTICE DIRECTION 23A – INTERNATIONAL PROTECTION OF ADULTS

This practice direction supplements Part 23 of the Court of Protection Rules 2017

General

1. This practice direction is made under rule 23.1(2) (which enables a practice direction to make additional or supplementary provision in respect of any of the matters set out in Part 23), and makes provision in relation to Schedule 3 applications.

The Convention

2. Schedule 3 of the Act makes reference to "the Convention". This is defined by paragraph 2 of Schedule 3 and section 63 of the Act as the Convention on the International Protection of Adults signed at the Hague on 13 January 2000. The Convention was ratified by the United Kingdom on 5th November 2003, but only for Scotland: the Convention has not been ratified for England and Wales. Paragraphs 8, 9, 19(2) and (5), Part 5, and paragraph 30 of Schedule 3 to the Act have effect only if the Convention is in force in accordance with Article 571 and it has been held2 that it is not: those provisions are accordingly treated as having no effect.

1 Paragraph 35 of Schedule 3 to the Act.

2 *Re PO* [2013] EWCOP 3932.

Definitions

3. Subject to paragraphs 4 to 6, words that are defined in the Act or the Rules have the same meaning in this practice direction.

4. *"Country":* Paragraph 3(1) of Schedule 3 to the Act defines "country" as including a territory which has its own system of law. For the purposes of the Act, the Rules and this practice direction, Scotland and Northern Ireland are considered to be foreign countries, as are (amongst others) British Overseas Territories and Crown Dependencies.

5. *"Lasting power":* Paragraph 13(6) of Schedule 3 to the Act defines "lasting power" as—

   (a) a lasting power of attorney within the meaning of section 9 of the Act

   (b) an enduring power of attorney within the meaning of Schedule 4, or

   (c) any other power of like effect.

6. For the purposes of Part 23 a power which would be a lasting power under paragraph 13(6) of Schedule 3 is excluded from the definition of "lasting power" if (a) it is a lasting power of attorney within the meaning of section 9 of the Act, or (b) it is an enduring power of attorney within the meaning of Schedule 4 of the Act (Rule 23.2(2) provides for the exclusion of such lasting powers from the scope of Part 23). In this practice direction "lasting power" has the same meaning as in Part 23.

Procedure for making a Schedule 3 application

7. A Schedule 3 application is to be made in accordance with Part 9 of the Rules subject to the modifications set out in this practice direction.

8. A Schedule 3 application is made by filing a COP 1 application form. The form shall be completed on the footing that the adult to whom the application relates is "P" for the purposes of the form. (Rule 23.3(1) provides for the provisions of the Rules to apply to Schedule 3 applications as if references therein to "P" were references to "the adult").

9. Notwithstanding the terms of Practice Direction 9A, an applicant making a Schedule 3 application is not required to file—

   (1) a COP 3 assessment of capacity form

   (2) any of the annexes listed in Practice Direction 9A

unless the applicant is also asking the Court to make additional declarations and / or orders under sections 15 and / or 16 of the Act, in which case the applicant should also file a COP 3 assessment of capacity form and such annexes as the applicant would have been required to file had he or she been seeking only those declarations and / or orders under sections 15 and / or 16 of the Act.

10. An applicant making a Schedule 3 application should identify whether any person other than the adult has an interest in the application such that they should be named as a respondent to it. For example where a Schedule 3 application is being made in relation to a lasting power it will usually be appropriate to name the donees of the power as respondent (unless they are themselves the applicants).

11. Rule 9.10 and Practice Direction 9B (requirement to notify other individuals) shall not apply to a Schedule 3 application unless the

applicant is also asking the Court to make additional declarations and / or orders under sections 15 and / or 16 of the Act, in which case the applicant should also notify such persons as the applicant would have been required to notify had he or she been seeking only those declarations and / or orders under sections 15 and / or 16 of the Act.

12. A Schedule 3 application should be accompanied by a COP 24 witness statement by or on behalf of the applicant. The evidence filed in support of the application should include—

(1) Where the application is made under rule 23.4 for recognition and / or enforcement of a protective measure under paragraph 20 or 22 of Schedule 3 to the Act:

(i) Evidence to demonstrate the basis upon which it is said that the person to whom the application relates is an adult for the purposes of Schedule 3 of the Act;

(ii) An officially authenticated copy (and where necessary a certified translation) of the relevant court order or other document embodying the protective measure in respect of which recognition and / or enforcement is sought;

(iii) Confirmation that the protective measure was taken on the basis that the adult was habitually resident in the other jurisdiction;

(iv) Evidence to enable the Court to be satisfied—

(i) that the case in which the measure was taken was urgent; alternatively

(ii) that the adult to whom the protective measure related was given an opportunity to be heard by the foreign court or other body that took the protective measure.

(v) Evidence to enable the court to be satisfied that the steps leading to the protective measure being made complied with any relevant provisions of the European Convention on Human Rights.

(vi) Details of any previous measures relating to the adult which have been the subject of a previous Schedule 3 application (whether or not such application was successful)

(vii) Where enforcement is sought of a protective measure that has already been recognised by the Court, a copy of the order giving effect to that recognition.

(2) Where the application is made under rule 23.5 to disapply or modify a lasting power under Schedule 3 of the Act or under rule 23.6 for declarations as to the authority of the donee of a lasting power, a certified copy of the lasting power (and where necessary a certified translation thereof).

Procedure after Issue

13. A Schedule 3 application is an excepted application for purposes of Practice Direction 3B (Case Pathways – see Part 1, paragraph 1.1 of that practice direction).

14. When a Schedule 3 application is issued the application will be put before a judge to give directions. The judge will case manage the application and decide whether to allocate it to a pathway. Specifically the judge will consider whether to make one or more of the directions set out in rule 1.2(2) to enable the adult to whom it relates to participate in the application or to secure the adult's interests and position.

15. Where the judge considers that the adult should be joined as a party to the proceedings the judge will direct the filing of a COP 3

Assessment of Capacity form or other expert evidence directed at the issue of the adult's capacity to conduct the proceedings before the Court. (Rule 23.3(2) provides for the issue of the adult's capacity to conduct the proceedings before the Court to be determined by reference to Part 1 of the Act).

16. An application under rule 23.4 for recognition and / or enforcement of a protective measure should be dealt with rapidly, and in reviewing the papers the Court will consider whether the order sought can be made without holding a hearing.

17. A Schedule 3 application under rule 23.4 for recognition and / or enforcement of a protective measure which—

(1) purports to authorise a deprivation of liberty of the adult to which it relates (other than a temporary or transient deprivation of liberty associated with the transfer of the adult to or from a specified place); or

(2) purports to authorise medical treatment

will usually—

(1) be determined after holding a hearing; and

(2) be allocated to the Senior Judge or a Tier 3 Judge.

Applications involving issues of habitual residence

18. An application in which the Court is being asked to make a declaration that a person is habitually resident in England and Wales for the purposes of exercising its jurisdiction under sections 15 and / or 16 of the Act is not a Schedule 3 application for the purposes of the Rules or this practice direction unless an order under rules 23.4 to 23.6 is being sought within the application.

19. No determination as to a person's habitual residence is required in order for the court to hear an application under section 21A of the Act, although a determination may be required if the court is then invited to exercise its jurisdiction under sections 15 and / or 16 of the Act.

20. Where an application (whether or not a Schedule 3 application) seeks declarations as to a person's habitual residence the Court will in case managing the application have regard to ensure that the application is allocated to an appropriate level of judge.

APPENDIX C

PRACTICE DIRECTION 9H – PROPERTY AND AFFAIRS DEPUTYSHIP APPLICATIONS

This practice direction supplements Part 9 of the Court of Protection Rules 2017

1. This Practice Direction is made under rule 9.11. It provides a different procedure for making property and affairs deputyship applications such that P and people to be notified of the application are notified and invited to indicate their consent or objection before the application is issued.

2. Subject to paragraph 2A, applications falling within this Practice Direction may be filed online through the portal for making property and affairs deputyship applications available on the Court of Protection.gov.uk website ("the online portal"), where such use is agreed by the court as practicable.

2A. With effect from 2 December 2024 and subject to paragraph 2B, use of the online portal is mandatory where the application is filed by any person who, by filing the application on behalf of the applicant, is acting in a professional capacity or for remuneration. A failure to use the online portal where this is mandatory will usually result in the court determining that the applicant may not recover their costs of the application.

2B. In a case to which paragraph 2A applies, where the person filing an application is unable to use the online portal due to a requirement for reasonable adjustment due to disability, they should explain their need for a reasonable adjustment to the court. by means of a covering letter when making their application through any other permitted method

General

3. This Practice Direction applies only to applications for property and affairs deputyship orders. The rules and Practice Directions which apply to such applications continue to apply except where and to the extent that they are disapplied and different provision is made as set out in this Practice Direction. Where the provisions of this Practice Direction conflict with other provisions of the Rules or other Practice Directions, this Practice Direction will take precedence. Any application which has been started under the previous Practice Direction (Practice Direction 9H – Property and Affairs Deputyship Applications), shall continue under this Practice Direction, and any reference to COP14PADep and COP15PADep in this Practice Direction shall be read as including COP14Pilot and COP15Pilot for such applications.

4. In this Practice Direction the term "applicant" includes a person who intends to or has completed an application for a property and affairs deputyship order but has not yet issued it.

Notifying P that an application is going to be made

5. In relation to notifying P that an application for a property and affairs deputyship order is going to be made Rules 7.4(1)(a), 7.4(2) (Application form), 7.8(3) (Manner of notification), 7.9 (acknowledgement of notification), 7.10 (Certificate of notification), and 9.9 (Applicant to notify P of an application) do not apply.

6. Rule 7.11 applies with the words "paragraphs 7 and 8 of Practice Direction 9H" substituted for "the provisions in this Part" in rule 7.11(1)(a) and (b).

7. Save where an application is made under rule 7.11, before filing a completed application for a property and affairs deputyship with the court the applicant must notify P that the application is going

to be made using the notification form COP14PADep which provides the following information:

a. Who the applicant is;

b. That the application raises the question of whether P lacks capacity in relation to a matter or matters and what that means;

c. What will happen if the court makes an order or direction that has been applied for;

d. Details of the person it is proposed should be appointed to make decisions on behalf of P in relation to their property and affairs;

e. That P may seek advice and assistance in relation to the application;

f. That P may complete and return the form to the person notifying them to acknowledge notification and indicate their wishes and feelings about the application;

g. That the notification form must be returned to the applicant before the end of 14 days from the date P received it, and if it is not sent within this period the court will assume that P does not object;

h. That P may, in addition to sending the completed form back to the applicant, send a copy of it to the court;

i. That at the point the application is made, the applicant will be required to provide to the court a copy of the notification form if it has been completed and returned to the applicant; and The COP14PADep also contains a section to be completed by the person who personally notifies P, to record the steps taken to explain the application to P, the extent to which they understood or appeared to understand and any response they gave and any wishes and feelings P expressed about the application.

8. P must be provided with the information set out in paragraph 7 in a way that is appropriate to P's circumstances (for example using simple language, visual aids or any other appropriate means).

Persons to notify that an application is going to be made

9. Rule 9.10 does not apply.

10. Before filing a completed application for a property and affairs deputyship order with the court, the applicant must give notice to any proposed respondent and to the persons to be notified (being those persons that are required to be notified of an issued application as specified in Practice Direction 9B) that an application is going to be made using the notification form COP15PADep which provides the following information:

    a. Who the applicant is;

    b. Details about the person to whom the application relates (P);

    c. Details of the application being made and the order or orders sought;

    d. The full name and address of the person being notified and their connection to P;

    e. That the person notified is asked to complete the form and return it to the applicant no more than 14 days after receiving it, to acknowledge notification and to indicate whether they consent or object to the application;

f. That the person may, in addition to sending the completed form back to the applicant, send a copy of it to the court; and

g. That at the point an application is made, the applicant is required to provide to the court all completed notification forms where these have been returned to the applicant within the prescribed time.

Responding to notice that an application is going to be made

11. (a) A person notified that an application is going to be made pursuant to paragraph 10 above should complete the notification form COP15PADep and return it to the applicant before the end of 14 days from the date of receipt, indicating whether they consent or object to the proposed application.

(b) The person to whom the application relates may complete the COP14PADep and the applicant must return the form to the court if the person to whom the application relates completes it.

(c) If a person notified that an application is going to be made fails to return the completed notification form COP14PADep or COP15PADep to the applicant by the end of 14 days from receipt, the applicant can make the application with a declaration that no response has been received, and the court will infer that there is no objection to it.

(d) If a person notified that an application is going to be made objects to the application, the person notified may, in addition to sending the completed notification form COP14PADep or COP15PADep to the applicant, file a copy of the completed form directly with the court.

Timing of the application

12. The applicant must not file the application with the court until either:

    a. they have received acknowledgment of notification from all persons notified,

    or

    b. the end of 14 days after the latest notification was provided pursuant to paragraphs 7 and 10 above, whichever is the earlier.

13. Where the applicant has not filed the application with the court by the end of three months after first notifying any person that an application is going to be made, the applicant must provide new notification in accordance with paragraphs 7 and 10 above before filing the application with the court.

Filing the application: using the online portal or other method permitted by the Rules

14. To file an application with the court using the online portal the applicant must:

    a. complete the form in the online portal, providing the following information which is signed with a statement of truth and an acknowledgement that the court may contact any of the persons listed:

        (i) the date on which P was notified and steps taken to enable P to understand the information;

        (ii) Details of any wishes and feelings expressed by P about the application;

(iii) Details of the people notified that the application was going to be made, and their relationship to P;

(iv) the dates on which each person was notified or an explanation as to why they have not been notified;

(v) whether the persons notified consent or object to the application or have not responded; and

b. upload all completed acknowledgement of notification forms received;

c. upload all supporting documents as required by Rule 9.4 and Practice

Direction 9A; and

d. Pay the appropriate court fee (with professional users using Payment by Account where possible).

15. To file an application otherwise than using the online portal, the applicant must file

with the court:

a. the completed COP1 which is signed with a statement of truth and an acknowledgement that the court may contact any of the persons listed:

(i) Details of the people notified that the application was going to be made, and their relationship to P;

(ii) the dates on which each person was notified or an explanation as to why they have not been notified;

(iii) whether the persons notified consent or object to the application or have not responded; and

b. the completed COP14PA Dep providing the date on which P was notified, steps taken to enable P to understand the information, and any wishes and feelings expressed by P about the application;

c. all completed acknowledgement of notification forms received;

d. all supporting documents as required by Rule 9.4 and Practice Direction 9A;

and

e. Pay the appropriate court fee (with professional users using Payment by Account where possible).

Online Portal

16. If there are technical difficulties with the online portal such that court receives an incomplete form or application or there are difficulties accessing some or all of the uploaded documents, the court will contact the applicant and invite them to rectify the errors.

Issue of application

17. When the court receives a complete form and application in accordance with paragraphs 14-16 above, it must issue the application, and notify the applicant of the date of issue.

After the application has been issued

18. Rule 9.6 does not apply.

19. As soon as practicable after issue of the application an Authorised Court Officer will consider the application, including the following matters:

    a. whether the applicant has complied with the requirements of this practice direction and in particular whether further consideration of the application needs to be deferred in accordance with paragraph 20 below;

    b. whether the court requires any additional information regarding notification that the application was going to be made;

    c. whether the application contains any request under rule 7.11 or otherwise in relation to dispensing with the requirement to serve or notify any person of the application prior to issue; and

    d. whether any person served or notified of the application has indicated that they object or has failed to respond (which will include consideration of any completed notification forms COP14PADep or COP15PADep received by the court direct from a person notified) and may as appropriate, request additional information, defer further consideration, issue case management directions and/or refer the matter to a judge under paragraph 22, or make the order requested in accordance with paragraph 21.

20. Applications which do not attach completed acknowledgement of notification forms from all persons notified, and which have been filed before the end of the 14 day period following the latest notification provided pursuant to paragraphs 7 and 10 above, will not be further considered by an Authorised Court Officer before 14 days from the date of issue of the application.

21. Applications in which all persons notified that the application was going to be made have indicated their consent to the order sought or have failed to respond within the prescribed time and such time having now expired, will be treated as uncontested applications and considered on the papers by an Authorised Court Officer.

22. Paragraph 2.2 of Practice Direction 2B applies with the following modifications:

    a. where any person notified that an application is going to be made has indicated that they object to it, or seek a different or additional order, an Authorised Court Officer may make standard directions to:

        (i) allocate the application to the Property and Affairs pathway set out in Part 3 of Practice Direction 3B – Case Pathways;

        (ii) join any person objecting to the proposed order as a respondent to the matter, and join any other person as a party where appropriate;

        (iii) provide for service of the application, supporting documents and the directions order on any respondent;

        (iv) provide for any respondent to file reasons for the objection;

        (v) provide for the listing of a dispute resolution hearing; and

        (vi) require costs details of each party to be available at the dispute resolution hearing.

b. where the court officer considers that the application is complex or contentious for any reason beyond the notification of an objection, that additional or alternative directions should be made or that for any other reason it is appropriate, they must refer the matter to a judge for consideration and for directions to be made which may include (but are not limited to) all of those listed in subparagraphs (i) to (vi) ab

APPENDIX D

PRECEDENT ORDER APPOINTING A PROPERTY AND AFFAIRS DEPUTY

IN THE COURT OF PROTECTION

No.

MENTAL CAPACITY ACT 2005

IN THE MATTER OF

[NAME]

ORDER APPOINTING A DEPUTY FOR

PROPERTY AND AFFAIRS

Made by

At

On

UPON the Court being satisfied that [name] lacks capacity to make various decisions for [himself] [herself] in relation to a matter or matters concerning [his] [her] property and affairs, and that the purpose for which this order is needed cannot be effectively achieved in a way that is less restrictive of [his] [her] rights and freedom of action.

AND UPON the Court being satisfied that [name]'s interests and position can be properly secured without being joined to these proceedings and without making any further direction concerning [name]'s participation in these proceedings.

IT IS ORDERED THAT

1. Appointment of [deputy] [joint deputies]

(a) [N [s] and address[es] [is] [are] appointed [jointly] [jointly and severally] as [deputy] [deputies] [("the deputy")] [("the deputies")] to make decisions on behalf of [name] that [he] [she] is unable to make for [himself] [herself] in relation to [his] [her] property and affairs, subject to any conditions or restrictions set out in this order.

(b) The appointment will last until further Order.

(c) The [deputy] [deputies] must [jointly and severally] apply the principles set out in section 1 of the Mental Capacity Act 2005 ("the Act") and have regard to the guidance in the Code of Practice to the Act.

2. Authority of [deputy] [deputies]

(a) The court confers general authority on the [deputy] [deputies] to take possession or control of the property and affairs of [name] and to exercise the same powers of management and investment as [he] [she] has as beneficial owner, subject to the terms and conditions set out in this order.

(b) The [deputy] [deputies] cannot purchase any freehold or leasehold property on [name]'s behalf without obtaining further authority from the court.

(c) The [deputy] [deputies] must not sell, charge or otherwise dispose of any freehold or leasehold property in which [name[has a joint beneficial interest. An order authorising the appointment of a new trustee (or trustees) in place of [name] must be obtained before any sale or disposition of the property.

(d) If the [deputy] [deputies] consider it in [name]'s best interests to do so the deputy may appoint an investment manager, who is regulated and authorised to undertake investment business, to manage [his] [her] assets on a discretionary basis under the standard terms and conditions applicable to such service from to-to-time, and to permit the investments to be held in the name of the investment manager nominee company.

(e) The [deputy] [deputies] may make provision for the needs of anyone who is related to or connected with [name] if [he] [she] provided for, or might be expected to provide for, that person's needs by doing whatever [he] [she] did, or might reasonably be expected to do, to meet those needs.

(f) The [deputy] [deputies] may (without obtaining any further authority from the court) dispose of [name]'s money and property by way of gift to any charity to which [he] [she] made, or might have been expected to make, such gifts, and, on customary occasions, to persons who are related to or connected with [him] [her], provided that the value of each such gift is not unreasonable having regard to all the circumstances and, in particular, the size of [his] [her] estate.

(g) For the purpose of giving effect to any decision the [deputy] [deputies] may execute or sign any necessary deeds or documents.

3. Reports

(a) The [deputy is] [deputies are jointly] required to keep statements, vouchers, receipts and other financial records.

(b) The [deputy must] [deputies must jointly] submit an annual report to the Public Guardian as and when required to do so.

4. Costs and expenses

The [deputy is] [deputies are] authorised to pay [law firm] fixed costs for this application, or, where the amount exceeds the fixed costs allowed, the [deputy is] [deputies are] authorised to agree the costs for making this application and to pay them from funds belonging to [name]. In default of agreement, or if the deputy or the solicitors would prefer the costs to be assessed, this order is to be treated as authority to the Senior Court Costs Office to carry out a detailed assessment on the standard basis.

6. Security

(a) The [deputy is] [deputies are jointly] required forthwith to obtain and maintain security in the sum of £[sum] in accordance with the standard requirements as to the giving of security.

(b) The [deputy] [deputies] must ensure that the level of security ordered by the court is in place before discharging any of the functions conferred by this order.

7. Notification

The [deputy] [deputies] must, within 14 days of service of this order by the court, notify [name] personally that the court has made a decision by providing [him] [her] with a notice of proceedings about you in the Court of Protection (form COP14) and a copy of this Order. The requirement for the person effecting notification of the issue of this order to provide the court with a certificate of notification is dispensed with.

8. Right to apply for reconsideration of order

This order was made without a hearing and without notice. Any person affected by this order may apply within 21 days of the date on which this order was served to have the order set aside or varied pursuant to Rule 13.4 of the Court of Protection Rules 2017 ("the Rules"). Such application must be made on Form COP9 and in accordance with Part 10 of the Rules.

APPENDIX E

PRECEDENT ADDITIONAL AUTHORITY CLAUSES FOR A PROPERTY AND AFFAIRS DEPUTYSHIP ORDER

Authority of deputy/ies

- A declaration that P lacks mental capacity to manage his or her affairs

- To confer general authority on the [deputy] [deputies] to take possession or control of the property and affairs of [name] and to exercise the same powers of management and investment, as [he] [she] has as beneficial owner

- The [deputy] [deputies] may make provision for the needs of anyone who is related to or connected with [name] if [he] [she] provided for, or might be expected to provide for, that person's needs by doing whatever [he] [she] did, or might reasonably be expected to do, to meet those needs

- The [deputy] [deputies] may (without obtaining any further authority from the court) dispose of [name]'s money and property by way of gift to any charity to which [he] [she] made, or might have been expected to make, such gifts, and, on customary occasions, to persons who are related to or connected with [him] [her], provided that the value of each such gift is not unreasonable having regard to all the circumstances and, in particular, the size of [his] [her] estate

- For the purpose of giving effect to any decision the [deputy] [deputies] may execute or sign any necessary deeds or documents

- To authorise the [deputy] [deputies] to sell the property of [name] known as [address of property] on the best possible terms and after payment of legal fees and other professional charges to invest the net proceeds for [name]'s benefit

- To authorise the [deputy] [deputies] to purchase and freehold or leasehold property on [name]'s behalf without obtaining further authority of the court

- Authority for the [deputy] [deputies] to take such steps as may be necessary to obtain (either alone or with a co-administrator) a grant of representation to the estate of [name] and to use the share to which [name] is entitled for [his] [her] benefit

- The [deputy is] [deputies are] authorised to pay [law firm] fixed costs for this application, or, where the amount exceeds the fixed costs allowed, the [deputy is] [deputies are] authorised to agree the costs for making this application and to pay them from funds belonging to [name]. In default of agreement, or if the deputy or the solicitors would prefer the costs to be assessed, this order is to be treated as authority to the Senior Court Costs Office to carry out a detailed assessment on the standard basis.

- The [deputy is] [deputies are] authorised, with retrospective effect as necessary, to instruct [name] to advise and assist in respect of issuing arising in connection with [detail]. In order to give effect to this authority, the [deputy is] [deputies are] authorised to use funds of [name] up to a limit of £[amount]. (For the avoidance of doubt, this authority does not extend to the issue or conduct of proceedings in respect of [name].)

- In so far as the authority granted by paragraph [number] above is retrospective, the costs already incurred by the [deputy] [deputies] shall be subject to detailed assessment by the Senior

Courts Costs Office on the standard basis. The [deputy is] [deputies are] authorised to make from the funds of [name] a payment on account not exceeding 75% + VAT of the total sum authorised in paragraph [number] above, pending assessment.

- The [deputy is] [deputies are] authorised to obtain Counsel's opinion (including by conference, and including paying the costs of attendance at such conference by [name]) on matters relating to [name]. In order to give effect to this authority the [deputy is] [deputies are] authorised to use funds of [name] up to a total limit of £[amount].

- To authorise the [deputy] [deputies] to conduct proceedings in the name of and on behalf of [name] and to act therein in litigation friend in relation to [detail]

- To authorise the [deputy] [deputies] to act as litigation friend for [name] in the divorce and financial remedies proceedings and to approval any financial settlement

- To authorise the [deputy] [deputies] to conduct proceeds as litigation friend in the name of and on behalf of [name] under the Inheritance {Provision for Family and Dependents) Act 1975

- The [deputy] [deputies] be authorised to realise £[amount] by entering into an equity release scheme over the property known as [address] and prepare a trust deed to protect [name]'s beneficial interest in the property

- The [deputy] [deputies] be authorised in the name of and on behalf of [name] [jointly with] to enter into a mortgage of the [jointly owned] property with [lender] and to execute any necessary documents

APPENDIX F

PRECEDENT ORDER AUTHORISING A DEPUTY TO DEAL WITH ASSETS ABROAD

IN THE COURT OF PROTECTION

No.

MENTAL CAPACITY ACT 2005

IN THE MATTER OF

[NAME]

ORDER

Made by

At

On

WHEREAS

(1) By an order dated [date] [name] ("the deputy") was appointed as deputy for property and affairs for [name].

(2) An application has been made by [name] for authority to sell the property situated at [address] as well as for authority to deal with [name]'s financial affairs in [country].

2. The Court being satisfied that [name] lacks capacity to make various decisions for [himself] [herself] in relation to a matter or matters concerning [his][her] property and affairs, and that the purpose for which this order is needed cannot be effectively achieved in a way that is less restrictive of [his][her] rights and freedom of action.

AND UPON the Court being satisfied that [name]'s interests and position can be properly secured without being joined to these proceedings and without making any further direction concerning [name]'s participation in these proceedings.

IT IS ORDERED THAT

1. Further authority of deputy

   a. The deputy is authorised to take such steps as are necessary or expedient in accordance with the laws of [country] to take possession or control of the property and affairs of [name] in [country].

   b. Subject to the laws of [country], the deputy is authorised to sell the property situated at [address] ("the Property").

   c. The deputy is authorised to deal with any bank accounts, pension policies or other assets or accounts that are situated in [country] and held in [name]'s sole name [or the joint names of [name] and [name]].

   d. Provided that the duties and function of the deputy are not delegated, the deputy is authorised, provided that it is also in the best interests of [name], to appoint any other necessary third party to enable the deputy to exercise any powers under the Court of Protection order dated [date] to assist with the sale of the Property and the general management of [name]'s property and financial affairs in [country]. For the avoidance of doubt this is to include the appointment of a lawyer, notary, translator, accountant, real estate agent and/or other professionals and to settle the fair and reasonable costs of these professionals from the estate of [name].

e. Authority to take investment advice in [country] and authority to repatriate any proceeds of assets held in [country] to England and Wales to be managed in accordance with the terms of the Court of Protection order dated [date].

f. For the purpose of giving effect to any decision the deputy may execute or sign any necessary deeds or documents relating to [name]'s property and financial affairs in [country]. For the avoidance of doubt this is to include any deed or document needed to facilitate the sale of the Property as well as any bank accounts, pension policies or any other assets or accounts that are situated in [country] and are held in [name]'s sole name [or the joint names of [name] and [name]].

g. The reasonable costs of any necessary travel by the deputy to [name] for the purposes of executing or signing any deed or document that is needed to facilitate the sale of Property shall be paid from the estate of [name].

2. Costs and expenses

a. The cost of this application is to be paid from [name]'s assets and fixed at [amount] plus VAT and disbursements but if the costs exceed the fixed amount they may be subject to a detailed assessment on the standard basis. This order is to be treated as an authority to the Senior Court Costs Office to assess these costs.

b. For the avoidance of doubt, any professional fees or disbursements incurred by the deputy in acting under the terms of this order are to be paid from estate of [P] and this order is to be treated as authority to the Senior Court Costs Office to assess these costs on the standard basis.

3. Right to apply for reconsideration of order

This order was made without a hearing and without notice. Any person affected by this order may apply within 21 days of the date on which this order was served to have the order set aside or varied pursuant to Rule 13.4 of the Court of Protection Rules 2017 ("the Rules"). Such application must be made on Form COP9 and in accordance with Part 10 of the Rules.

APPENDIX G

PRECEDENT ORDER AUTHORISING THE DEPUTY TO TRANSFER P'S PROPERTY TO A FOREIGN APPOINTED REPRESENTATIVE AND DISCHARGING THE DEPUTY

IN THE COURT OF PROTECTION

No.

MENTAL CAPACITY ACT 2005

IN THE MATTER OF

[NAME]

ORDER

Made by

At

On

WHEREAS

(1) By an order dated [date] [name] ("the deputy") was appointed as deputy for property and affairs for [name].

(2) An application has been made by the deputy for an order under the Mental Capacity Act 2005 to discharge [his][her] deputyship.

(3) The court has considered the information provided by the deputy as to the remaining assets of [name] held in England and Wales [following the transfer of [name]'s funds to [name] acting on behalf of [name].

(4) The court is satisfied that there is no longer a requirement for [name] to have a deputy acting on [his][her] behalf in relation to [his][her] property and affairs in England and Wales.

IT IS ORDERED THAT

1. The deputy is forthwith to transfer all property belonging to [name] which remains under [his][her] control to [name], the [name of country] legal representative acting on behalf of [name]. Whereupon the deputy is discharged from the deputyship and her powers are terminated.

2. Any funds in court, and any funds held elsewhere, are to be transferred forthwith to [name], the [name of country] legal representative on behalf of [name], or as they shall direct.

3. [The deputy shall file a final account with Public Guardian by [date] and if approved by the Public Guardian may seek the discharge of her security.]

4. Any outstanding costs of general management are to be agreed and paid by [P]. In default of agreement, or if [P] or the solicitors would prefer the costs to be assessed, this order is to be treated as authority to the Senior Courts Costs Office to carry out a detailed assessment on the standard basis.

5. This order was made without a hearing and without notice. Any person affected by this order may apply within 21 days of the date on

which this order was served to have the order set aside or varied pursuant to Rule 13.4 of the Court of Protection Rules 2017 ("the Rules"). Such application must be made on Form COP9 and in accordance with Part 10 of the Rules.

APPENDIX H

RE UR [2021] EWCOP 10

IT IS DECLARED PURSUANT TO SECTION 15 OF THE MENTAL CAPACITY ACT 2005 THAT:

1. It is lawful, as being in UR's best interests, to be transported from AL Nursing Home to East Midlands Airport in accordance with the transition plan attached to this order and to thereafter reside with her sister and niece within the Polish property. For the avoidance of doubt, UR:

(5) Has a reasonable excuse to leave AL Nursing Home as she falls (directly or implicitly) within the exemptions contained in paragraph 2(2)(f)(iv), paragraph (5)(c) and (e), paragraph (7) and/or paragraph 13 of schedule 3A(1) of the Regulations, or

(6) Otherwise has reasonable excuse to leave the UK in accordance with the finding of this court that it is in her best interests to do so; recognising that the exemptions set out in paragraph 2 of schedule 3A(1) of the Regulations are not exhaustive by application of paragraph 1(2)(a) of schedule 3A(1) of the Regulations.

IT IS ORDERED PURSUANT TO SECTION 16(1)(a) AND SECTION 16(2)(a) AND BEING A RELEVANT DECISION UNDER SECTION 4A(3) AND (4) OF THE MENTAL CAPACITY ACT 2005 AND THEREBY PERMITTING UR's DEPRIVATION OF LIBERTY, AND IF AND TO THE EXTENT THAT SHE IS SO DEPRIVED:

2. It is lawful and in UR's best interests to be transported from AL Nursing Home to East Midlands Airport in accordance with the transition plan attached to this order and to thereafter reside with her

sister and niece within the Polish property. To the extent that the restrictions in place during the transportation constitute a deprivation of her liberty, such deprivation is authorised by the court.

3. In the event that it is necessary, the Local Authority and CCG, by their employees or agents, may use reasonable and proportionate measures to transport UR from AL Nursing Home to East Midlands Airport which must be done in a way which is the least restrictive and consistent with UR's best interests and implemented in a way calculated to cause UR the least distress, and only such force as is necessary is used and that any safety restraint techniques are used only by persons having appropriate training. For the avoidance of doubt, the level of restraint relates to chemical sedation and not physical restraint.

THE COURT HAS DETERMINED PURSUANT TO SECTION 21A(2)(a) AND SECTION 21A(3)(b) OF THE MENTAL CAPACITY ACT 2005 THAT:

4. The best interests qualifying requirement is not met. In particular:

    (1) It is not in UR's best interests to continue to reside at AL Nursing Home and to receive a package of care therein in accordance with her assessed needs;

    (2) In order to prevent harm to UR, it is not necessary for her to reside at AL Nursing Home;

    (3) UR's continued residence at AL Nursing Home is not a proportionate response to the likelihood of her suffering serious harm if she were not a detained resident.

5. Upon UR leaving the jurisdiction of England and Wales, the Local Authority, in its capacity as the supervisory body, is directed to terminate the standard authorisation.

AND IT IS ORDERED THAT:

6. Permission is granted to the parties to jointly instruct Mr Tomasz Kurek of Kurek & Partners Law Office, Warsaw, Poland, to prepare the power of attorney and to thereafter make the necessary application to the Voivode to confirm UR's Polish citizenship. The court approves 1-2 hours of work at a cost of between £100-200 plus 23% VAT for the preparation of the power of attorney and 10-15 hours of work at a cost of £1,000-1,500 plus 23% VAT for the application to be made to the Voivode. Such cost shall be apportioned equally between the parties and is a necessary expense upon UR's public funding certificate.

7. The Local Authority and CCG shall, forthwith, take the necessary steps to ensure that the transition plan [E/96-90] and, upon completion, an updated care plan (prior to her discharge from AL Nursing Home) are translated into Polish, and for copies to be thereafter provided to UR's sister and niece. The transition plan will be provided to UR's sister and niece within 4 weeks of the date of this order, and the updated care plan within 2 weeks of it being completed. Any costs in relation to such translation are to be borne equally by the Local Authority and CCG.

8. Upon UR leaving the jurisdiction of England and Wales, these proceedings shall conclude.

9. The solicitor for the Local Authority has permission to disclose a copy of this order to AL Nursing Home.

10. The Local Authority shall ensure that a copy of this order is provided to its DoLS team.

11. The CCG shall ensure that a copy of UR's medical records (hospital and GP) are provided to any health and social care provider in Poland (which is/ will be providing health and social care to UR in

Poland) upon being notified of the names/ addresses of any providers.

12. Liberty to any party to apply at 48 hours' notice to the court and the other parties to vary or set aside any of the terms of this order on a general basis. Additionally, if UR indicates a wish to return to the UK during the 3-day window staff are with her in Poland and lacks capacity to make the decision to return to England, an urgent hearing will be required which will need to consider (inter alia) whether UR remains habitually resident in England and Wales. Any application so made shall be reserved to Mr Justice Hayden.

13. This order takes effect when made, whether or not it bears the seal of the court.

14. No order as to costs, save for a detailed assessment of the costs of UR who is a legally aided party.

MORE BOOKS BY LAW BRIEF PUBLISHING

A selection of our other titles available now:-

'A Practical Guide to Probation Breaches and Other Applications' by Mark Thomas
'A Practical Guide to Remarriage and Divorce' by Cordelia Williams & Claire Howard
'A Practical Guide to Privacy, Transparency, Reporting Restrictions and Closed Proceedings in the Court of Protection' by Laura Mannering
'Beaumont on Barristers – A Guide to Defending Disciplinary Proceedings (Second Edition)' by Marc Beaumont
'A Practical Guide to Payments for Environmental Services' by Ben Sharples
'A Practical Guide to the Law of Pregnancy and Maternity at Work' by Rebecca Thomas
'A Practical Guide to Redundancy – Second Edition' by Philip Hyland & Collette Moore
'A Practical Guide to International Issues for Scottish Family Lawyers' by Susie Mountain, Donna McKay, Ken MacDonald
'A Practical Guide to the Law on Deprivation of Liberty' by Ben Troke
'A Practical Guide to Rights over Airspace and Subsoil – Second Edition' by Daniel Gatty
'A Practical Guide to the Law in Relation to Inquests' by Ramya Nagesh
'A Practical Guide to the Construction and Rectification of Wills and Trust Instruments (Second Edition)' by Edward Hewitt
'A Practical Guide to Data Protection in Social Housing' by Clare Paterson
'A Practical Guide to Spousal Maintenance – Second Edition' by Liz Cowell
'A Practical Guide to International Parental Child Abduction Law (England and Wales)' by Dr Onyója Momoh
'A Practical Guide to Deprivation of British Citizenship' by Sean Ell
'A Practical Guide to Commercial Property Service Charges' by Rachel Garton
'A Practical Guide to Clinical Negligence – Third Edition' by Geoffrey Simpson-Scott (Geoff)
'A Practical Guide to the Rights of Grandparents in Children Proceedings – Second Edition' by Stuart Barlow

‘The Electronic Communications Code: A Practical Guide – Second Edition’ by Kerry Bretherton KC, James Castle, Mark Loveday

‘A Practical Guide to the Independent School Standards – September 2023 Edition’ by Sarah McKimm

'A Practical Guide to Estate Administration and Crypto Assets' by Richard Marshall

‘A Practical Guide to Parental Alienation in Private and Public Law Children Cases’ by Sam King QC & Frankie Shama

‘Contested Heritage – Removing Art from Land and Historic Buildings’ by Richard Harwood QC, Catherine Dobson, David Sawtell

‘The Limits of Separate Legal Personality: When Those Running a Company Can Be Held Personally Liable for Losses Caused to Third Parties Outside of the Company’ by Dr Mike Wilkinson

‘A Practical Guide to Transgender Law’ by Robin Moira White & Nicola Newbegin

‘A Practical Guide to ‘Stranded Spouses’ in Family Law’ by Mani Singh Basi

‘A Practical Guide to Residential Freehold Conveyancing’ by Lorraine Richardson

‘A Practical Guide to Pensions on Divorce for Lawyers’ by Bryan Scant

‘A Practical Guide to Challenging Sham Marriage Allegations in Immigration Law’ by Priya Solanki

‘A Practical Guide to Digital Communications Evidence in Criminal Law’ by Sam Willis

‘A Practical Guide to Legal Rights in Scotland’ by Sarah-Jane Macdonald

‘A Practical Guide to New Build Conveyancing’ by Paul Sams & Rebecca East

‘A Practical Guide to Inherited Wealth on Divorce’ by Hayley Trim

‘A Practical Guide to Practice Direction 12J and Domestic Abuse in Private Law Children Proceedings’ by Rebecca Cross & Malvika Jaganmohan

‘A Practical Guide to Confiscation and Restraint’ by Narita Bahra QC, John Carl Townsend, David Winch

‘A Practical Guide to the Law of Forests in Scotland’ by Philip Buchan

‘A Practical Guide to Health and Medical Cases in Immigration Law’ by Rebecca Chapman & Miranda Butler

‘A Practical Guide to Bad Character Evidence for Criminal Practitioners by Aparna Rao

‘A Practical Guide to Extradition Law post-Brexit’ by Myles Grandison et al

‘A Practical Guide to Hoarding and Mental Health for Housing Lawyers’ by Rachel Coyle

'Stephens on Contractual Indemnities' by Richard Stephens
'A Practical Guide to the EU Succession Regulation' by Richard Frimston
'A Practical Guide to Solicitor and Client Costs – Second Edition' by Robin Dunne
'Constructive Dismissal – Practice Pointers and Principles' by Benjimin Burgher
'A Practical Guide to Religion and Belief Discrimination Claims in the Workplace' by Kashif Ali
'A Practical Guide to the Law of Medical Treatment Decisions' by Ben Troke
'Fundamental Dishonesty and QOCS in Personal Injury Proceedings: Law and Practice' by Jake Rowley
'A Practical Guide to the Law in Relation to School Exclusions' by Charlotte Hadfield & Alice de Coverley
'A Practical Guide to Divorce for the Silver Separators' by Karin Walker
'The Right to be Forgotten – The Law and Practical Issues' by Melissa Stock
'A Practical Guide to Planning Law and Rights of Way in National Parks, the Broads and AONBs' by James Maurici QC, James Neill et al
'A Practical Guide to Election Law' by Tom Tabori
'A Practical Guide to the Law in Relation to Surrogacy' by Andrew Powell
'A Practical Guide to Claims Arising from Fatal Accidents – Second Edition' by James Patience
'A Practical Guide to Asbestos Claims' by Jonathan Owen & Gareth McAloon
'A Practical Guide to Stamp Duty Land Tax in England and Northern Ireland' by Suzanne O'Hara
'A Practical Guide to the Law of Farming Partnerships' by Philip Whitcomb
'A Practical Guide to the Law of Unlawful Eviction and Harassment – Second Edition' by Stephanie Lovegrove
'A Practical Guide to Costs in Personal Injury Claims – Second Edition' by Matthew Hoe
'A Practical Guide to the General Data Protection Regulation (GDPR) – Second Edition' by Keith Markham
'A Practical Guide to Working with Litigants in Person and McKenzie Friends in Family Cases' by Stuart Barlow
'Protecting Unregistered Brands: A Practical Guide to the Law of Passing Off' by Lorna Brazell
'A Practical Guide to Secondary Liability and Joint Enterprise Post-Jogee' by Joanne Cecil & James Mehigan

'A Practical Guide to the Pre-Action RTA Claims Protocol for Personal Injury Lawyers' by Antonia Ford
'A Practical Guide to Neighbour Disputes and the Law' by Alexander Walsh
'A Practical Guide to Coercive Control for Legal Practitioners and Victims' by Rachel Horman
'A Practical Guide to the Law of Driverless Cars – Second Edition'
by Alex Glassbrook, Emma Northey & Scarlett Milligan
'A Practical Guide to TOLATA Claims' by Greg Williams
'A Practical Guide to Elderly Law – Second Edition' by Justin Patten
'A Practical Guide to Responding to Housing Disrepair and Unfitness Claims' by Iain Wightwick
'A Practical Guide to the Law of Bullying and Harassment in the Workplace' by Philip Hyland
'How to Be a Freelance Solicitor: A Practical Guide to the SRA-Regulated Freelance Solicitor Model' by Paul Bennett
'A Practical Guide to Prison Injury Claims' by Malcolm Johnson
'A Practical Guide to Advising Clients at the Police Station' by Colin Stephen McKeown-Beaumont
'A Practical Guide to Antisocial Behaviour Injunctions – Second Edition' by Iain Wightwick
'Practical Mediation: A Guide for Mediators, Advocates, Advisers, Lawyers, and Students in Civil, Commercial, Business, Property, Workplace, and Employment Cases' by Jonathan Dingle with John Sephton
'The Mini-Pupillage Workbook' by David Boyle
'A Practical Guide to Crofting Law' by Brian Inkster
'A Practical Guide to the Law of Domain Names and Cybersquatting' by Andrew Clemson
'A Practical Guide to the Law of Gender Pay Gap Reporting' by Harini Iyengar
'NHS Whistleblowing and the Law' by Joseph England
'Employment Law and the Gig Economy' by Nigel Mackay & Annie Powell
'A Practical Guide to Noise Induced Hearing Loss (NIHL) Claims' by Andrew Mckie, Ian Skeate, Gareth McAloon
'An Introduction to Beauty Negligence Claims – A Practical Guide for the Personal Injury Practitioner' by Greg Almond
'Intercompany Agreements for Transfer Pricing Compliance' by Paul Sutton
'Zen and the Art of Mediation' by Martin Plowman
'A Practical Guide to Adoption for Family Lawyers' by Graham Pegg

'A Practical Guide to Industrial Disease Claims' by Andrew Mckie & Ian Skeate
'A Practical Guide to Conducting a Sheriff Court Proof' by Andrew Stevenson
'A Practical Guide to Vicarious Liability' by Mariel Irvine
'A Practical Guide to Applications for Landlord's Consent and Variation of Leases' by Mark Shelton
'A Practical Guide to Relief from Sanctions Post-Mitchell and Denton' by Peter Causton
'A Practical Guide to Equity Release for Advisors' by Paul Sams
'A Practical Guide to Financial Services Claims' by Chris Hegarty
'A Practical Guide to Financial Ombudsman Service Claims' by Adam Temple & Robert Scrivenor
'A Practical Guide to Running Housing Disrepair and Cavity Wall Claims – Second Edition' by Andrew Mckie & Ian Skeate
'A Practical Guide to Holiday Sickness Claims – Second Edition' by Andrew Mckie & Ian Skeate
'Arguments and Tactics for Personal Injury and Clinical Negligence Claims' by Dorian Williams
'A Practical Guide to Drone Law' by Rufus Ballaster, Andrew Firman, Eleanor Clot
'On Experts: CPR35 for Lawyers and Experts' by David Boyle
'An Introduction to Personal Injury Law' by David Boyle

These books and more are available to order online direct from the publisher at www.lawbriefpublishing.com, where you can also read free sample chapters. For any queries, call us on 0844 587 2383 or email us at mail@lawbriefpublishing.com.

Our books are all generally in stock at www.amazon.co.uk with free next day delivery for Prime members, and at good legal bookshops such as Wildy & Sons.

We are regularly launching new books in our series of practical day-to-day practitioners' guides. Visit our website and join our free newsletter to be kept informed and to receive special offers, free chapters, etc.

You can also follow us on Twitter at www.twitter.com/lawbriefpub.

www.ingramcontent.com/pod-product-compliance
Lightning Source LLC
LaVergne TN
LVHW022056200926
848481LV00003B/942
* 9 7 8 1 9 1 8 2 4 1 3 2 7 *